Kevin Clancy is a partner and solicitor-advocate at Shepherd and Wedderburn. For over a decade, he has advised and represented clients at Licensing Boards and Licensing Committees throughout Scotland.

A trusted adviser to his clients, Kevin has experience of dealing with routine and contentious hearings in relation to liquor licences, taxi and private hire licences, public entertainment licences, houses in multiple occupation licences, and late hours catering licences.

For the past two years Kevin has been advising clients regarding the consultation, legislation, and implementation stages of the new Short-term Lets Licensing Scheme.

A Practical Guide to the Short-Term Lets Licensing Scheme in Scotland

A Practical Guide to the Short-Term Lets Licensing Scheme in Scotland

Kevin Clancy

Solicitor-Advocate

LL.B (Hons), DipLP

Law Brief Publishing

© Kevin Clancy

All rights reserved. No part of this publication may be reproduced, stored in a retrieval system, or transmitted, in any form or by any means, electronic, mechanical, photocopying, recording or otherwise, without the prior permission of the publisher.

Excerpts from judgments and statutes are Crown copyright. Any Crown Copyright material is reproduced with the permission of the Controller of OPSI and the King's Printer for Scotland. Some quotations may be licensed under the terms of the Open Government Licence (http://www.nationalarchives.gov.uk/doc/open-government-licence/version/3).

Cover image © iStockphoto.com/Drimafilm

The information in this book was believed to be correct at the time of writing. All content is for information purposes only and is not intended as legal advice. No liability is accepted by either the publisher or author for any errors or omissions (whether negligent or not) that it may contain. Professional advice should always be obtained before applying any information to particular circumstances.

Published 2023 by Law Brief Publishing, an imprint of Law Brief Publishing Ltd
30 The Parks
Minehead
Somerset
TA24 8BT

www.lawbriefpublishing.com

Paperback: 978-1-914608-75-9

Dedicated to Samantha and Sophia

PREFACE

Licensing law, in all of its forms, is a very interesting subject and a deeply rewarding field in which to practice. The technicalities of the written law (not always conveniently found in the one Act of Parliament) frequently have to be balanced against persuasive advocacy before licensing boards and committees, taking into account the ultimate practical goal (securing a client's licence on the best terms possible).

Short-term letting licensing is the newest recruit to the various types of civic licence that can be granted under the Civic Government (Scotland) Act 1982.

In this practical guide, I have attempted to draw together the many and varied sources of information on short-term letting – legislation, guidance documents, policy advice notes, and other commentary – in order to assimilate in one place the key issues that will face hosts, operators, platforms, licensing officers and practitioners. I have included footnote references to legislation and guidance, but references to case law have been kept deliberately light. I have also tried to keep the text concise. I recognise that is a lofty aspiration!

In order to keep this book to a manageable length, it has required a slightly selective approach, but I hope that by focusing on what are likely to be the more interesting issues – planning permission, control areas, the application process, and compliance – this book does achieve its ambition of being a practical guide.

As will inevitably be the case with new legislation in its formative weeks and months, unexpected issues may crop up or aspects of the licensing scheme will be subject to judicial challenge. The introduction of the licensing scheme on 1 September 2022 is certainly not the last word on the matter.

My thanks go to my publishers, Tim Kevan and Garry Wright, for their encouragement in making sure an idea became a reality, and to my Dad for having critiqued earlier drafts of the text.

I have endeavoured to state the law as I understood it to be as at 31 December 2022.

Kevin Clancy
December 2022

CONTENTS

Chapter One	Historical Context	1
	Introduction	1
	Key Legislation	1
	Expert Panel on the Collaborative Economy and Short-Term Lets Delivery Group	2
	Consultations, consultations, consultations…	3
	Legislating for the 2022 Order	6
	Purpose of the licensing scheme	7
Chapter Two	Short-Term Lets: Basic Principles	9
	Introduction	9
	Basic components of the definition of a short-term let	9
	Further criteria to be applied to the basic components	12
	Immediate Family Members	13
	Qualifying relationships/relatives	14
	Excluded Accommodation	14
	Practical Considerations for Excluded Accommodation	16
	Excluded Tenancies	19
Chapter Three	Rules of the Game for Making an Application	21
	Introduction	21
	New Host or Existing Host?	21
	Phase 1: From 1 October 2022	22
	Phase 2: From 1 October 2023	24
	Phase 3: From 1 July 2024	25

	Practical Considerations	25
	What type of licence is required?	26
Chapter Four	The Interaction Between Planning Law and Licensing Law	29
	Introduction	29
	Certificate of Lawfulness of Existing Use or Development	30
	Short-term let control areas	30
	What might provoke a control area designation?	31
	Effect of designation	33
	Practical Considerations – short-term let control areas	34
	City of Edinburgh Council	34
	Highland Council	39
	Planning Permission under the 2022 Order	41
	Existing Hosts making an application prior to 1 October 2023	42
	Preliminary refusal: breach of planning control	43
	Practical Considerations	45
	Further planning guidance	45
	City of Edinburgh Council	46
	Glasgow City Council	48
	Perth and Kinross Council	49
	What if a short-term let control area is subsequently introduced to my local authority area?	50
Chapter Five	The Mandatory Conditions (And Additional Conditions)	53
	Introduction	53
	The mandatory conditions and practical considerations	54

	Additional licence conditions		66
		Conditions potentially caught by existing legislation	67
		Refuse	68
		Maintenance and other costs	69
		Hot tubs, spa pools, etc	69
		Carpets	70
		Miscellaneous conditions: decks, speakers and window opening restrictors...	71
Chapter Six	Can I Let Out Short-Term Properties on a Temporary Basis?		73
	Introduction		73
	Temporary Licences		74
	Temporary Exemption		76
Chapter Seven	The Application Process		79
	Introduction		79
	The relevant licensing authority		79
	Layout plans		82
	Applicants		84
	Owner Consent		85
	Day-to-day managers		85
	Publicity		85
	Objections and representations		87
	Disposal of applications for grant and renewal of licence		88
	The licensing hearing		89
	Grounds of refusal		91
	Licence duration		95
	Deemed grant of a licence application		98

	Changes and alterations	99
	Surrender of licence	100
	Public register	101
	Giving of Reasons	103
	Appeals	104
Chapter Eight	**Compliance**	**109**
	Introduction	109
	What might enforcement look like?	109
	Enforcement notices	110
	Variation, suspension or revocation of the licence	110
	Criminal liability	113
	Operating without a licence	113
	Failing to comply with a licence condition	114
	Making a false statement	115
	Failing to notify a change	116
	Further consequences	117
	Practical considerations	118
Chapter Nine	**Looking to the Future**	**121**

CHAPTER ONE

HISTORICAL CONTEXT

Introduction

1.1   Short-term lets provoke political debate, local disagreement, and occasional controversy. From relatively humble beginnings – one well-known booking platform can trace its origins back to advertising air mattresses to rent – it is now a global billion-dollar industry.

1.2   The popularity of short-term lets in Scotland has soared in recent years, most notably in three local authorities: the City of Edinburgh Council, the City of Glasgow Council and Highland Council. But, it is a divisive topic. The number of hosts and guests may have continued to increase, but so too has political opposition. The administration at Edinburgh Council has made its position quite clear in recent years – it has taken the view that for far too long, too many homes have been lost in the city to the holiday market[1].

Key legislation

1.3   At a national level, the Scottish Government has viewed the issue as being worthy of legislation. There are two key pieces of legislation that will be referred to in this book – the Civic Government (Scotland) Act 1982 (which will be referred to as **the 1982 Act** for ease) and the Civil Government (Scotland) Act 1982 (Licensing of Short-term Lets) Order 2022 (which will be referred to as **the 2022 Order** for ease). Those reading this book who have experience in civic licensing matters (such as taxi

---

[1]   Edinburgh to become first short-term let control area in Scotland – The City of Edinburgh Council

licensing, public entertainment licensing, etc) will be well familiar with the 1982 Act. That Act sets out the framework by which licensing applications should be applied for and determined. Although the 2022 Order is a new legislative instrument, the new short-term licensing scheme will be implemented with reference to both the 1982 Act and the 2022 Order.

1.4 From a position of relatively no regulation to the introduction of the 2022 Order, it has not been a smooth journey for the Scottish Government. That formal regulation of short-term lets is needed at all is because the Government considered that the short-term letting of properties had become more accessible than ever before. Perhaps even too accessible. Of course, one cannot ignore the benefits to Scotland's economy brought about by short-term lets. However, the Government wished to balance the economic advantages against concerns that existed about the growth in the numbers of short-term lets. It is a complicated conundrum, in which (i) increasing tourism and economic growth, (ii) reversing depopulation and staff shortages in rural hospitality, and (iii) limited housing stock for a local community that is becoming more irritated by "stag and hen do tourism", are all competing interests.

Expert Panel on the Collaborative Economy and Short-Term Lets Delivery Group

1.5 To begin our legislative journey, we must go back to April 2017 when the Scottish Government set up the Expert Panel on the Collaborative Economy. The Panel was set the task of identifying how Scotland could maximise the benefits of the collaborative economy, whilst overcoming challenges that might stand in the way (economic and social challenges, but underpinned by regulation that was fit for purpose).

1.6 Around a year later, the Short-Term Lets Delivery Group (with representation across areas such as housing, licensing, planning, tax, etc) was established with a solutions-focused approach to the question of short-term lets. In addition to gathering relevant evidence, the Group also sought to identify what existing powers local authorities already had to combat this issue. Put another way, it was in nobody's interest to double regulate the same issue.

Consultations, consultations, consultations…

1.7   In April 2019, the Scottish Government launched a public consultation[2] and commissioned independent research[3] into the impact of short-term lets on people and communities. The consultation paper considered the available evidence as regards short-term lets, not only in Scotland but also further afield. This was in the context of the consultation paper referencing its understanding that there may be upwards of 21,000 short-term listings in Scotland. (Pausing there: on the – perhaps unlikely – hypothesis that all hosts and operators of existing short-term let premises apply for a short-term let licence, can it be said that the relevant stakeholders are sufficiently resourced to deal with what might be described as a tsunami of licence applications – will licensing authorities have staff numbers to cope? Will Police Scotland have the resources to report on every application? What about the fire service and other enforcement officers? Even allowing for the likelihood that a significant proportion of hosts and operators may leave the short-term let sector and return to the private landlord sector, this will still be a considerable workload for licensing authorities to deal with.)

1.8   It was at this point that the possibility of licensing short-term lets was first raised as part of the wider discussion as to what sort of regulatory approach would be appropriate and proportionate. An alternative that was considered (and strongly supported by industry bodies), but ultimately not taken forward, was a

---

[2] Short-term lets: consultation – gov.scot (www.gov.scot)

[3] Short-term lets: consultation annexes – gov.scot (www.gov.scot)

registration system (such as had already been implemented on the continent – as in the Netherlands).

1.9   The consultation (the first of three) was reported on in October 2019[4], the consultation having received over 1,000 responses. This was accompanied by research to assess the positive and negative impacts of short-term lets[5].

1.10 In parallel with the consultation, what is now the Planning (Scotland) Act 2019 completed its passage through the Scottish Parliament and included provision for the establishment of short-term let control areas[6]. The planning implications of the new short-term lets regime are discussed in more detail in chapter 4.

1.11 The start of 2020 then saw the Scottish Government bring forward several proposals in consequence of the consultation response and the independent research. There was a commitment to consider how short-term lets would be financially taxed, and to empower local authorities to introduce short-term let control areas. However, the headline announcement was the proposal to establish a licensing scheme (and not a registration scheme) for short-term lets. This would not be an entirely new or radical piece of legislation; rather, the licensing scheme would use powers that already existed under the 1982 Act. Addressing what was perceived to be a significant gap with the *status quo*, the licensing scheme would include mandatory safety requirements which would apply to all short-term lets across Scotland.

1.12 The COVID-19 pandemic then struck in March 2020, which only served to delay matters by several months. Indeed, it was only towards the end of 2020 (September) that the Scottish

---

[4] Short-term lets consultation: response analysis – gov.scot (www.gov.scot)

[5] Short-term lets – impact on communities: research – gov.scot (www.gov.scot)

[6] Section 17 of the Planning (Scotland) Act 2019, introducing a new section 26B to the Town and Country Planning (Scotland) Act 1997

Government launched its second consultation – this time introducing a working definition of short-term lets. Detailed documents were also published setting out what such a licensing scheme might look like. As before, a report to the consultation was published in December 2020[7] after having received over 1,000 responses. The intention had been to bring a licensing scheme into effect by April 2021, and the rationale in imposing mandatory safety standards was that it would mean a level playing field for all short-term lets.

1.13 There were then a couple of twists and turns at this juncture. The then Minister for Local Government, Housing and Planning (Kevin Stewart MSP) laid regulations at the Scottish Parliament which would have given short-term letting licensing the force of law (together with the Control Area Regulations and the Business and Regulatory Impact Assessment). That was in December 2020. In what could only be described as a complete U-turn, the proposed Licensing Order was withdrawn in February 2021. That was (at least in part) as a consequence of widespread criticism and concern from various stakeholders. The withdrawal of the proposed Licensing Order would also give the Scottish Government time to provide draft guidance on the licensing scheme. Given the proximity of the Scottish elections in May, the issue was effectively parked for several months (albeit the Scottish Government still managed to ensure that regulations legislating for short-term let control areas were approved by the Scottish Parliament, and came into force on 1 April 2021 – more on that in chapter 4).

1.14 By June 2021, a third consultation was launched[8]. This was much more narrowly focused on what was then a revised draft

---

[7] Short-term lets – licensing scheme and planning control areas: consultation analysis – gov.scot (www.gov.scot)

[8] Short-term Lets: Consultation on draft Licensing Order and Business and Regulatory Impact Assessment (BRIA) – Scottish Government – Citizen Space

Licensing Order and getting the implementation of a licensing scheme correct. This led, on 7 October 2021, to the Cabinet Secretary for Social Justice, Housing and Local Government (Shona Robison MSP) announcing what were said to be a number of pragmatic changes[9]. For example, regulations designed to prevent "overprovision" were to be removed from the scheme; there was to be a reduction in the public liability insurance requirements; there would be focused use of inspections and stronger guidance on fees; publicity and notification requirements would be simplified. By the end of November 2021, a new Licensing Order was laid before Parliament.

Legislating for the 2022 Order

1.15   The result of this was the approval of the 2022 Order by the Scottish Parliament on 19 January 2022, and which came into force on 1 March 2022. Local authorities had until 1 October 2022 to establish a licensing scheme (which has been done). As will be discussed in Chapter 3, there are then various deadlines for applying for and obtaining a short-term let licence. All hosts and operators must have a licence by 1 July 2024.

1.16   In order to help hosts, booking platforms, local authorities and others better understand how the 2022 Order should be interpreted and implemented, the Scottish Government has published guidance documents in two parts (and which will be referred to throughout this book). **Part 1** is directed towards Guidance for Hosts and Operators[10]. **Part 2** is directed towards Licensing Authorities, Letting Agencies and Booking

---

[9]   Cabinet Secretary for Social Justice Housing and Local Government (www.gov.scot)

[10] Short-term Lets in Scotland Licensing Scheme: Part 1 Guidance for Hosts and Operators (www.gov.scot)

Platforms[11]. Both guidance documents should be considered essential reading for anyone involved in dealing with short-term let licence applications (which will be referred to as **Part 1** or **Part 2 of the Guidance** for ease).

Purpose of the licensing scheme

1.17 The stated purpose in the Scottish Government guidance of this new licensing scheme is "to ensure basic safety standards are in place across all short-term lets operating in Scotland"[12]. More specifically, the aims of the licensing scheme are stated to be[13] :

- To ensure all short-term lets are safe

- To facilitate licensing authorities in knowing and understanding what is happening in their area

- To assist with handling complaints and address issues faced by neighbours effectively.

1.18 Ensuring all short-term lets are safe is a laudable aim of a new licensing scheme. However, as we will discuss in Chapter 4, the actual implementation of licensing policy by local authorities risks confusing licensing issues (regulation and safety) with policy concerns that are more truly within the domain of the planning authorities. To the extent any part of a licensing policy introduced by a licensing authority does go beyond its licensing function, it introduces the possibility that the policy is vulnerable to judicial review or appeal in what is known as the *Brightcrew*

---

[11] Short-term Lets in Scotland Licensing Scheme: Part 2 Supplementary Guidance for Licensing Authorities, Letting Agencies and Platforms (www.gov.scot)

[12] Para 1.9, SG Guidance Part 1

[13] Para 1.10, SG Guidance Part 1

sense[14], or any individual decision on a licensing application is vulnerable to appeal. Licensing authorities will be well advised to remember that distinction.

1.19 For those looking for even more "light" reading on the subject, useful background information can be found in the report of the consultation on the draft Licensing Order[15] and the Business and Regulatory Impact Assessment[16], both published on 23 November 2021.

1.20 With that overview of the background to, and context for, the 2022 Order, the first important question to address is what is (and what is not) a short-term let?

---

[14] An appeal under the Licensing (Scotland) Act 2005 in the case of *Brightcrew Limited v The City of Glasgow Licensing Board* [2011] CSIH 46: Para 26: *The fact that the objectives listed in … the 2005 Act are all desirable in a general sense does not empower a licensing board to insist on matters which, while perhaps unquestionably desirable in that sense, are nevertheless not linked to the sale of alcohol. For a licensing board so to insist would be to divert a power from its proper purpose.*

[15] Short-term lets – draft Licensing Order and business and regulatory impact assessment: consultation report – gov.scot (www.gov.scot)

[16] Short-term lets: business and regulatory impact assessment – gov.scot (www.gov.scot)

CHAPTER TWO

SHORT-TERM LETS: BASIC PRINCIPLES

Introduction

2.1 Probably the most important question that operators, booking platforms, licensing authorities, and solicitors will require to consider is this: what is meant by a short-term let?

2.2 That is both in terms of properties that will now be caught by the short-term let definition (and thus require to be licensed) but also, just as crucially to those involved in the renting of residential property, those properties that will be considered "excluded" from the scope of the 2022 Order. This question is set against a background context of an incredible variety of properties now available for residential accommodation, from the grandeur of a castle, through to serviced apartments, through to yurts! A full and proper understanding of the new legislation is essential.

2.3 You might be forgiven for thinking that the statutory description of a short-term let would be relatively straight-forward. Not so. The meaning of a short-term let requires careful consideration of various statutory definitions, all of which are set out below.

Basic components of the definition of a short-term let

2.4 We begin with what might be described as the basic components, or building blocks, of a short-term let definition. The key definition can be found in Article 3 of the 2022 Order.

2.5 There are five basic components to the definition, <u>all of which need to apply</u> when a host or operator is considering whether or not to apply for a licence. Those are:

- *The use of residential accommodation*, which includes the whole or part of a premises (unless it is an "excluded" accommodation or tenancy).

    This covers the full spectrum of conventional and unconventional accommodation types. For example, this could be a single room, a whole house (perhaps even a castle!), a guesthouse, a B&B or hotel (unless a licence under the Licensing (Scotland) Act 2005 is required), a boathouse, a chalet, a farmhouse, a caravan or a glamping pod (unless a caravan site licence is required), a tent, treehouse, or even a yurt!

    A licence will be required for each premises that is let out. However, a distinction needs to be drawn between the *premises* (for which a licence is required) and the *accommodation* contained within the premises.

    Why is that distinction important? It is possible you could have more than one accommodation on a single premises, but that would only require a single short-term let licence[17]. For example, two apartments, cottages or chalets will likely require two licences, but a field (premises) containing ten wigwams or multiple rooms separately let out in the one house or apartment will require only one licence.

- *Provided by a host*, who is defined as a person who is the owner, tenant, or person who otherwise exercises control over occupation and use, of the accommodation which is the subject of a short-term let[18].

---

[17] Article 4 of the 2022 Order

[18] Article 2 of the 2022 Order

SHORT-TERM LETS: BASIC PRINCIPLES

- *In the course of business* (and for commercial consideration). No distinction should be drawn between whether a guest is staying for leisure or work purposes. Both might be considered a short-term let. Rather, the question is whether there has been an arrangement in the course of business (for example, online bookings) where the host advertises available residential accommodation, and the guest accepts terms and conditions that apply to the booking.

    The terms and conditions of the residential accommodation are important. It is very unlikely that you are engaged in short-term let activity if the property is truly offered for free. That said, if the accommodation is provided for free, but the guest is providing the host with work, or a service, or goods **all in lieu of payment**, or **there is a reciprocal arrangement in place** (for example, a holiday house swap) then the premises and the activity could potentially be considered as a short-term let requiring a licence.

    It does not matter how long a guest wishes to stay – a short-term let can be measured by one night, or even several months, provided the rest of the statutory criteria is met.

- *To a guest*, being the person who occupies accommodation under a short-term let.

- *And where certain further criteria are met.*

2.6 A fairly common question that arises when hosts contemplate the use of residential accommodation is the extent to which any of what is set out above interacts with existing legislation in place to licence Houses of Multiple Occupation (HMO). Using residential accommodation for the purpose of a private residential tenancy would not bring short-term let licensing into play (since that would be considered an Excluded Tenancy). However, for those landlords operating a HMO (for which a HMO licence is required), it is important to be aware that only having the HMO

11

licence is not sufficient if you also offer short-term lets within the HMO – a short-term let licence **AND** a HMO licence will be required.

Further criteria to be applied to the basic components

2.7   These basic components are then built upon by the further criteria in Article 3 of the 2022 Order, all of which require to be met:

> (a) *the guest does not use the accommodation as their only or principal home* (it could be said this is the primary point of distinction between a short-term let accommodation and other traditional tenancies, or accommodation for which a HMO licence would be required),
>
> (b) *the short-term let is entered into for commercial consideration* – that includes money and a benefit in kind (such as provision of a service, or reciprocal use of accommodation – although a distinction should be drawn between a guest providing a modest "thank you" gift, which would not be commercial consideration, and a guest providing more substantial goods in lieu of a payment of money, which would likely be an agreement in the course of business),
>
> (c) *the guest is not*—
>
>> (i) *an immediate family member of the host,*
>>
>> (ii) *sharing the accommodation with the host for the principal purpose of advancing the guest's education as part of an arrangement made or approved by a school, college, or further or higher educational institution, or*
>>
>> (iii) *an owner or part-owner of the accommodation (for example, a time-share in specific accommodation, although an owner or part-owner of that accommodation thereafter letting out the*

accommodation to a guest would be a short-term let requiring a licence),

(d) *the accommodation is not provided for the principal purpose of facilitating the provision of work or services by the guest to the host or to another member of the host's household (such as live-in care arrangements or the guest is staying for the purpose of their work),*

(e) *the accommodation is not excluded accommodation, and*

(f) *the short-term let does not constitute an excluded tenancy.*

2.8 The further criteria that is applied to the basic building blocks also needs to be read in conjunction with various definitions that are provided for by Article 2 of the 2022 Order:

Immediate family members[19]

2.9 What does it mean to be "an immediate family member"?

A person ("A") is an immediate family member of another person ("B") if A is—

(a) *in a qualifying relationship with B,*

(b) *a qualifying relative of B,*

(c) *a qualifying relative of a person who is in a qualifying relationship with B, or*

(d) *in a qualifying relationship with a qualifying relative of B.*

---

[19] Article 2 of the 2022 Order

Qualifying relationships/relatives[20]

2.10   What then of a "qualifying relationship" or a "qualifying relative" when considering the definition of "immediate family member"? Two people are in a qualifying relationship with one another if they are— (i) married to each other, (ii) in a civil partnership with each other, or (iii) living together as though they were married. A "qualifying relative" means a parent, grandparent, child, grandchild or sibling.

2.11   In terms of the definitions that exist as regards children and siblings, it is worth noting that two people are to be regarded as siblings if they have at least one parent in common. A person's stepchild is to be regarded as the person's child. Finally, a person ("C") is to be regarded as the child of another person ("D"), if C is being or has been treated by D as D's child.

Excluded accommodation

2.12   That covers all of the relevant definitions as regards short-term lets, as defined by the 2022 Order. It is important to also have regard to excluded accommodation and excluded tenancies. Indeed, the exclusions are just as interesting as the short-term let definitions.

2.13   Excluded accommodation[21] means accommodation which is, or is part of—

  (a) *an aparthotel,*

  (b) *premises in respect of which a premises licence within the meaning of section 17 of the Licensing (Scotland) Act 2005 has effect and where the provision of accommodation is an activity listed in the operating plan as defined in section 20(4)*

---

[20] Article 2 of the 2022 Order

[21] Schedule 1 to the 2022 Order

of that Act,

(c) *a hotel which has planning permission granted for use as a hotel,*

(d) *a hostel,*

(e) *residential accommodation where personal care is provided to residents,*

(f) *a hospital or nursing home,*

(g) *a residential school, college or training centre,*

(h) *secure residential accommodation (including a prison, young offenders institution, detention centre, secure training centre, custody centre, short-term holding centre, secure hospital, secure local authority accommodation, or accommodation used as military barracks),*

(i) *a refuge,*

(j) *student accommodation,*

(k) *accommodation which otherwise requires a licence for use for hire for overnight stays,*

(l) *accommodation which is provided by the guest,*

(m) *accommodation which is capable, without modification, of transporting guests to another location,*

(n) *a bothy, or*

(o) *accommodation owned by an employer and provided to an employee in terms of a contract of employment or for the better performance of the employee's duties.*

Practical Considerations for Excluded Accommodation

2.14   The definition of "excluded accommodation" invites some interesting discussion points. Five of them are worth examining in a little more detail.

   (a) Aparthotels. Although making up a relatively small proportion of the UK's total hospitality accommodation, aparthotels are growing in popularity – especially amongst families or those who are in need of a longer stay but would prefer a living environment that is more homely than a hotel room.

   For the purposes of the 2022 Order, there are two important definitions in order to properly understand if the property can benefit from the aparthotel exclusion. The first is the definition of "aparthotel" and the second is the definition of "serviced apartment".

   "Aparthotel" means a residential building containing serviced apartments where— (a) the whole building is owned by the same person, (b) a **minimum number of 5 serviced apartments** are managed and operated as a single business, (c) the building has a shared entrance for the serviced apartments, and (d) the serviced apartments **do not share an entrance with any other flat or residential unit within the building**.

   So, there is both a numerical restriction (minimum number of 5 serviced apartments owned by the same person) and a logistical restriction (the whole building need not be wholly dedicated to the aparthotel but there cannot be a shared entrance with other non-serviced apartments).

   "Serviced apartment" means a flat or residential unit in respect of which— (a) services are provided to guests (such as housekeeping, a telephone desk, reception, or laundry), (b) each flat or unit contains its own washing, cooking and dining facilities separate from each of the other flats or units, and (c) there is a management system in place to prevent anti-social behaviour and to impose limits in respect of the maximum occupancy of the flats or units.

(b) Licensed premises is another interesting category of potentially excluded premises. This has come up as a discussion point where a hotel or such like (holding a premises licence) also has within its grounds or, in close proximity, a small cottage, or inn, or other form of residential accommodation. Is a short-term let licence required for the smaller property, or is the premises licence for the main hotel enough to benefit from the short-term let licence "exclusion"?

Firstly, one of the premises must hold a premises licence issued under the Licensing (Scotland) Act 2005 (i.e. a licence permitting the sale of alcohol on the premises). Not only that, but the operating plan (one of the main components of the alcohol licence) must list "accommodation" as one of the activities forming part of the licence (plainly a hotel will certainly have such an activity on its operating plan, but a restaurant in almost all probability will not). Simply having a premises licence will not be enough if the operating plan does not provide for accommodation as an activity.

Secondly, the cottage, or inn, or other form of residential accommodation would need to be included in the layout plan (another key component of the licence) and thus form part of the premises licence. It would not be enough for the nearby hotel to be licensed, but with the cottage entirely detached from the premises licence. That would be a step too far, and would not engage the "excluded premises" accommodation.

Each premises will turn on its own unique set of circumstances, but it can be seen that there may be occasions when it is desirable to take steps to include within the alcohol licence (the operating plan and the layout plan) other forms of residential accommodation that sit within the alcohol licence-holder's grounds and so avoid the need to separately apply for and obtain a short-term let licence.

For example, in circumstances where you might have a hotel and self-catering resort, there will likely be good reasons why the licensed footprint of the resort is the hotel only, and does not extend into the grounds of the property where the self-catering properties are. However, with the introduction of the 2022 Order, there might now be equally compelling reasons why a licence-holder would submit a variation application seeking to amend the layout plan so that the licensed footprint covers the entirety of the grounds of the resort (both the hotel and the self-catering properties) – in which case, the licence-holder will hold one licence under the Licensing (Scotland) Act 2005, that licence is in respect of both the hotel and the self-catering properties, and that licence provides for accommodation as an activity on the operating plan, rather than having to potentially apply for multiple short-term let licences.

(c) Staff accommodation. This issue often crops up, albeit not exclusively, in the context of more rural employment where living accommodation is (or requires to be) made available to the employee in terms of an employee's contract of employment or for the better performance of the employee's duties.

For example, where it can be shown that a flat or cottage owned by a hotel employer (perhaps in the Outer Hebrides) forms part of an employment package to entice a General Manager or other staff to the premises, then no short-term licence is going to be required.

(d) Very unorthodox and unusual accommodation. These will likely be excluded from the short-term let licensing regime – for example, a canal boat, or where the guest has to provide their own accommodation (such as a tent).

(e) Student accommodation. This is defined by the 2022 Order as "residential accommodation which has been built or converted predominately for the purpose of being provided to students"[22]. Premises that, for the majority of the year, are used as student accommodation (for example, halls of residence) may consider taking advantage of the way the legislation is expressed and rent out the accommodation to "guests" for weeks during the year outside of term time when there may be demand for a form of short-term letting. Those premises would be excluded from the requirement to hold a licence. By contrast, a flat that is let to students during the academic year may be an excluded tenancy (a student residential tenancy) but renting out the accommodation to guests over the summer months would require a short-term let licence.

Excluded Tenancies

2.15   Finally, to close off this chapter, it is worth considering what an "excluded tenancy"[23] is, being a tenancy which falls within any of the following definitions—

   (a)   *a protected tenancy (within the meaning of section 1 of the Rent (Scotland) Act 1984),*

   (b)   *an assured tenancy (within the meaning of section 12 of the 1988 Act),*

   (c)   *a short assured tenancy (within the meaning of section 32 of the 1988 Act),*

   (d)   *a tenancy of a croft (within the meaning of section 3 the 1993 Act),*

   (e)   *a tenancy of a holding situated outwith the crofting counties (within the meaning of section 61 of the 1993 Act) to which any provisions of the Small Landholders (Scotland) Acts,*

---

[22] Paragraph 3 to Schedule 1 of the 2022 Order
[23] Schedule 1 to the 2022 Order

1886 to 1931[1] apply,

(f) *a Scottish secure tenancy (within the meaning of section 11 of the 2001 Act),*

(g) *a short Scottish secure tenancy (within the meaning of section 34 of the 2001 Act),*

(h) *a 1991 Act tenancy (within the meaning of section 1(4) of the 2003 Act),*

(i) *a limited duration tenancy (within the meaning of section 93 of the 2003 Act),*

(j) *a modern limited duration tenancy (within the meaning of section 5A of the 2003 Act),*

(k) *a short limited duration tenancy (within the meaning of section 4 of the 2003 Act),*

(l) *a tenancy under a lease under which agricultural land is let for the purpose of its being used only for grazing or mowing during some specified period of the year (as described in section 3 of the 2003 Act),*

(m) *a private residential tenancy (within the meaning of section 1 of the 2016 Act), or*

(n) *a student residential tenancy.*

2.16 Looking at the issue in a very generalised manner, these definitions cover what most people would consider to be the traditional landlord and tenant relationship. If you have one of these agreements in place with a tenant, you will likely know about it. However, if there is any doubt, a conversation with your letting agent or solicitor would be recommended!

CHAPTER THREE

RULES OF THE GAME FOR MAKING AN APPLICATION

Introduction

3.1 By the time the stage has been reached that a short-term let licence application is to be made, hosts (or practitioners) will have done their homework to establish that (a) the premises concerned would fall within the short-term let definition and (b) the activity concerned requires a licence in terms of the 2022 Order. We have looked at both of those points in chapter 2. What next?

3.2 There are two further considerations for a host, operator, or practitioner – (i) what ***category*** of host is making the application and (ii) what ***type*** of short-term let is the application concerned with? The answers can be found by giving due consideration to both the 2022 Order and the Scottish Government guidance for Hosts and Operators.

3.3 In relation to the first question, it is the categorisation of the host that dictates the statutory timescales for applying for a licence as well as whether any short-term let activity may be undertaken whilst the licence application is pending.

New Host or Existing Host?

3.4 There are two options – whether the host is considered to be an "**existing host**" or a "**new host**". In order to answer that question, the key cut-off date is **1 October 2022**.

3.5 An existing host is "a host or operator who has used their premises to provide short-term lets before 1 October 2022 and who will apply for a licence to continue the same use"[24]. A new host is "a person or company that has not operated short-term lets at the premises they are applying for a licence for before 1 October 2022"[25].

3.6   The categorisation of the host and the 1 October 2022 cut-off is important because the licensing scheme has been brought into effect in three phases. When introducing the new licensing scheme, the Scottish Government presumably wished to avoid a cliff-edge whereby all existing short-term let activity ground to a halt whilst licensing authorities up and down the land furiously attempted to process the thousands (if not tens of thousands) of applications made under the new scheme. As such, transitional provisions (or saving provisions) were introduced to allow existing hosts to continue to trade if certain criteria were met.

Phase 1: From 1 October 2022

- *New hosts:* From 1 October 2022, a new host wishing to start letting out property for the first time must have a licence in place ***before*** taking bookings and receiving guests. Although it is permitted to advertise a short-term let, it is a criminal offence to take bookings and receive guests without first having a licence granted by the licensing authority.

- *Existing hosts:* If a host had let out property to guests prior to 1 October 2022 (i.e. the property has previously been used by guests on a short-term basis), the existing host has until **30 September 2023** to submit an application to the relevant licensing authority. If the existing host applies for a licence during this period, but the application is refused, the host must stop operating within 28 days (unless an appeal to the Sheriff Court is lodged within that time period, in which case the host may

---

[24] Section 7, Part 1 of the Guidance

[25] Section 7, Part 1 of the Guidance

continue to operate until such time as the appeal has been finally determined). In this context, finally determined means the application is granted or withdrawn, or the licensing authority refuses to consider the application for reasons relating to planning, or the application is refused by the licensing authority and no appeal is made within 28 days, or the application is refused by the licensing authority and appealed to the Sheriff Court (which is either abandoned or disposed of and all appellate options have been exhausted)[26].

3.7 It is worth observing at this point that, for existing hosts, the Scottish Government's original plan for the transition period was that existing hosts would have until 31 March 2023 to make an application for a short-term let licence. However, shortly before this book was finalised, the Scottish Government announced in December 2022 its plan to extend the deadline by which existing hosts need to apply for a licence (in order to continue operating as a host pending determination of that application) by six months **to 30 September 2023**. Although this is the Government's stated position, it will still be necessary for the Government to obtain legislative approval for this change from the Scottish Parliament. This book proceeds on the reasonable assumption that the Scottish Parliament will grant that approval, and that is likely to happen at some point in January 2023. Assuming the Parliament does give its approval, any historic references in this context to 31 March/1 April in already published materials should therefore be read as referring to 30 September/1 October 2023.

3.8 In her letter to the Convenor of the Local Government, Housing and Planning Committee on 7 December 2022, Shona Robison MSP explained that this would be a "one-off six-month extension recognising the wider economic circumstances of the cost-of-living crisis". Whilst the Cabinet Secretary for Social Justice,

---

[26] Article 7(8) and (9) of the 2022 Order

Housing and Local Government has explained the extension as being justified by the cost-of-living crisis, there must also be an element of licensing authorities and other stakeholders (such as Police Scotland, who will require to comment on each new application) simply not being ready for the rush of new applications that is likely to transpire. While the Scottish Government's proposal also has a very real practical advantage – existing hosts now know there has been a stay of execution on the need to apply for a short-term let licence until well after the summer festival events – there must be a very real risk that the Government's decision encourages existing hosts to do little about the licensing process at this time and instead prioritise bookings for the spring and summer seasons, resulting in licensing authorities being overwhelmed from September 2023 onwards by the volume of applications then made at that time.

Phase 2: From 1 October 2023

- *New hosts:* As before, if an applicant was not letting out property prior to 1 October 2022, the host must have a licence in place to accept bookings and receive guests.

- *Existing hosts:* To continue taking bookings and receiving guests after 1 October 2023 (previously 1 April 2023), the existing host must have submitted a licence application to the relevant licensing authority before 30 September 2023.

3.9 If an application has not been submitted by this date, the existing host cannot take bookings and receive guests until the licence has been granted (in other words, the licence application will be treated in the same way as for a new host).

3.10 If a licence application was lodged prior to 1 October 2023 but is then subsequently refused, the host must stop operating within 28 days (unless an appeal to the Sheriff Court has been lodged within that time period, in which case the host may continue to operate until such time as the appeal has been finally determined).

Phase 3: From 1 July 2024

- *All hosts:* By 1 July 2024, all hosts must have a licence in place to take bookings and receive guests.

Practical Considerations

3.11   It is unhelpful, I would suggest, that the definitions for existing host and new host are not in almost identical terms. As we discuss above, an existing host is someone who has *__used__* the premises for short-term letting before 1 October 2022, whereas a new host is someone that has not *__operated__* short-term lets prior to 1 October 2022. The two definitions are not identical, and indeed subtly different, albeit the importance of the distinction really only arises if there is ambiguity around whether a host or operator had been using premises for short-term letting on or around 1 October 2022.

3.12   For example, an existing host who has an established track record of bookings and payments prior to 1 October 2022 will have no trouble satisfying the existing host definition. It is to be expected that most (if not all) licensing authorities will operate a system of self-certification as to the existing host issue, but any applicant would be well advised to ensure it has evidence of prior bookings and payments should the licensing authority request proof that the applicant is properly considered to be an existing host.

3.13   What of a host or operator who had been gearing up for short-term letting, had advertised the property and accepted bookings (and, indeed, may have already accepted payment) prior to 1 October 2022, but who had not actually let out a room to a guest before 1 October 2022 (i.e. the bookings were only fulfilled at a point after 1 October 2022)? On one view, the premises was being *__operated__* as a short-term let (in the sense that bookings, for commercial consideration in the course of business, had been taken). On another view, the premises had certainly not been *used* as a short-term let by the operator or by guests prior to 1 October 2022.

3.14   It may be this is a typically legal analysis of definitions that have otherwise been drafted in order to be accessible to the layman. Licensing authorities may take a pragmatic view that provided the host had in some way operated as a short-term let prior to 1 October 2022 (and can evidence that), the host will be considered an existing host and so be permitted to take advantage of the more generous transitional provisions afforded to an existing host compared to a new host.

What type of licence is required?

3.15   Before applying for a licence you must determine what type of licence you require. There are four types of licences[27]:

   1. Licence for home sharing (where you let out part of your home to a guest who occupies the property along with you);

   2. Licence for home letting (where you let out your entire home while you are not occupying it);

   3. Licence for home sharing and home letting (a combination of licences 1 and 2 above); or

   4. Licence for secondary letting (where you have an additional property which you let out to guests).

3.16   As will become more apparent in later chapters, a far stricter approach is taken (by the 2022 Order and by licensing authority short-term let policies) towards secondary letting as opposed to home sharing or home letting.

---

[27] Paragraph 5 to Schedule 2 of the 2022 Order

3.17   In conclusion, I have described this chapter as the rules of the game for making an application. Unfortunately, there is not one rule book. Hosts and operators will require to be familiar with at least four documents:

1. the 2022 Order

2. the 1982 Act

3. the Scottish Government guidance

4. over and above those documents, the licensing scheme will be implemented by licensing authorities who will have prepared and published their own statements of short-term let licensing policy. It should be a fairly straight-forward task for a host to identify which licensing authority has jurisdiction over the short-term let application – it will be the licensing or regulatory committee within the local authority where the accommodation/premises are situated. For hosts who are operating premises across multiple local authority areas, unfortunately this means being familiar not just with the law and the guidance, but also multiple (and subtly different) licensing policies.

CHAPTER FOUR

THE INTERACTION BETWEEN PLANNING LAW AND LICENSING LAW

Introduction

4.1   To the uninitiated, it might not be immediately obvious why – in this form of civic licensing – planning law and licensing law are so interlinked. Indeed, a detailed consideration of planning law is beyond the scope of this book, and specialist advice should be sought. That said, the question of planning has caused such confusion amongst hosts and operators since the introduction of the 2022 Order that it is worth spending some time on.

4.2   The reason why planning law assumes importance in a licensing context is two-fold. Firstly, the 2022 Order empowers licensing authorities to suspend/refuse consideration of a short-term let licensing application if the licensing authority believes there has been a breach of planning control (with the licensing application process on hold until certain requirements have been satisfied)[28]. That involves an element of discretion on the part of the licensing authority, and brings into play subjective interpretations as to whether planning control matters are engaged. This could have an impact on home letting, home sharing, and secondary letting.

4.3   Secondly, the Scottish Government has legislated for what are known as **short-term let control areas**, and which are mandatory

---

[28] Article 7 of the 2022 Order (as it concerns applications by existing hosts) and paragraph 8 to Schedule 2 of the 2022 (as it concerns applications by new hosts, or by existing hosts who have missed the 30 September 2023 deadline)

in their effect. Control areas are targeted at only secondary letting.

4.4 As a general observation, it has always been the case that it is for a planning authority, on a case-by-case basis, to consider whether any change of use to a premises is material and therefore requires planning permission. It is probably fair to say, in the context of short-term letting, that over the last ten years or so the seeking out of planning permission has been more the exception rather than the rule.

Certificate of Lawfulness of Existing Use or Development

4.5 A final general, but very important, observation in the context of what follows is this – if premises have been used for short-term lets in a consistent manner for more than 10 years (without planning permission having been granted), one option (and a better option) for hosts and operators is to apply to the local authority for a **Certificate of Lawfulness of Existing Use or Development** to continue to operate the premises as such[29]. Applications for such a Certificate are not advertised, and there is no requirement to notify neighbours. The process is administratively far simpler than applying for planning permission. In terms of the 2022 Order when applying for a short-term let licence, if a licensing authority considers there has been a breach of planning control, then a licensing application can proceed with either (a) the grant of planning permission or (b) the grant of such a Certificate. For hosts who have been in the short-term let business for over 10 years, this is an important consideration to be aware of.

Short-term let control areas

4.6 The legislation underpinning Short-term let control areas pre-dates the coming into effect of the 2022 Order. Hosts and

---

[29] Section 150, Town and Country Planning (Scotland) Act 1997

practitioners will want to have regard to two pieces of linked legislation – the Town and Country Planning (Scotland) Act 1997 (**the 1997 Act**) and the Town and Country Planning (Short-term Let Control Areas) (Scotland) Regulations 2021 (**the 2021 Regulations**).

4.7　Dealing firstly with the key pieces of legislation and guidance: section 26B of the 1997 Act was introduced by section 17 of the Planning (Scotland) Act 2019. The 2021 Regulations were made under powers conferred by section 26B of the 1997 Act. Section 26B and the 2021 Regulations came into force on 1 April 2021, with a planning circular published on 25 June 2021[30] on guidance as to how a local authority can designate a control area.

4.8　A control area can be designated for one of the following reasons by a local authority[31]:

- To manage high concentrations of secondary letting where it affects availability of residential housing or neighbourhood character

- To restrict or prevent short-term lets in places/buildings where it is not appropriate

- To help local authorities ensure homes are put to best use in their areas.

What might provoke a control area designation?

4.9　Before an area can be designated as a short-term let control area, several criteria must first be met.

---

[30] Supporting documents – Planning circular 01/2021: short-term let control areas – gov.scot (www.gov.scot)

[31] Paragraph 2.8, Planning circular 01/2021: short-term let control areas

4.10 Firstly, the planning authority must give notice of the proposed designation. Secondly, the proposed designation must be approved by the Sottish Ministers. Thirdly, the planning authority must give notice of the designation[32].

4.11 The third pre-requisite – giving notice – is fairly self-explanatory. The second pre-requisite – that the designation must be approved by the Scottish Ministers – is interesting because very little guidance as to the process by which the Scottish Ministers should be considering and approving a proposed short-term let control area has been published. At present, only one local authority (the City of Edinburgh Council) has declared a short-term let control area. At the time of writing, one other (Highland Council) will almost certainly declare a short-term let control area. That is because Highland Council has completed steps (i) and (ii) of the three-step process. A short-term let control area for Badenoch and Strathspey has been proposed, with the Scottish Ministers approving the control area shortly before Christmas 2022. All that remains is for Highland Council to formally designate the area as such.

4.12 As for the first pre-requisite, the giving of notice is prescribed by Regulations[33]. The bigger question is: what might provoke a short-term let control area designation? Circumstances might include[34]:

- Changes to the look and feel of a neighbourhood, such as multiple key boxes on many buildings or structures or suitcase noise on streets and in stairwells.

---

[32] Regulation 3, Town and Country Planning (Short-term Let Control Area) Regulations 2021

[33] Regulation 4, Town and Country Planning (Short-term Let Control Area) Regulations 2021

[34] Paragraph 2.9, Planning circular 01/2021: short-term let control areas

THE INTERACTION BETWEEN PLANNING LAW AND LICENSING LAW

- Signs that local services are struggling, such as many instances of overflowing bins.

- Lack of affordable and appropriate housing for local residents.

- A significantly higher level of complaints relevant to use of dwellinghouses as short-term lets from neighbours.

- Detrimental impact on local amenity.

Effect of Designation

4.13   Planning permission is required where there is a material change of use in a building. Where an area has been designated as a short-term let control area, the use of a dwellinghouse for the purpose of providing short-term lets is **deemed** to involve a material change of use of the dwellinghouse[35]. Two observations can be made here:

   (i)   this deemed requirement of there being a material change of use only applies to **_secondary lettings_**. That is because, for the purposes of assessing material change of use for short-term lets, a tenancy of a dwellinghouse (or part of it) where all or part of the dwellinghouse is the only or principal home of the landlord or occupier[36] (in the language of short-term lets, that means home sharing or home letting accommodation) is excluded from the material change of use considerations.

   (ii) the short-term let material change of use considerations are defined as only impacting upon **_dwellinghouses_**. The Scottish Government has defined a dwellinghouse in its

---

[35] Section 26B(2), Town and Country Planning (Scotland) Act 1997
[36] Section 26B(3), Town and Country Planning (Scotland) Act 1997

Guidance as being "an independent dwelling (with its own front door, kitchen, and bathroom) such as a house, flat, cottage, etc". There will therefore be certain types of short-term lets, that are also secondary lets, for which a deemed material change of use will not arise.

4.14 The short point is this: once an area is designated as a control area, any use of a dwelling for <u>secondary letting</u> will be automatically deemed a material change in use. Therefore, this will require planning permission.

Practical Considerations – short-term let control areas

4.15 This book does not attempt to comment on all of the planning policies across the 32 local authorities. However, it is worth briefly considering at this stage the approach being taken to the issue by three local authorities – the City of Edinburgh Council, the Highland Council, and (in the next section) Glasgow City Council.

City of Edinburgh Council – Short-term let control area and changes to planning guidance

4.16 The City of Edinburgh Council has designated the whole of the local authority area as being a short-term let control area. As such, if you are the operator of a secondary letting dwellinghouse, the effect of the designation is that there has been a deemed material change of use. The consequence, in Edinburgh at least, is that every secondary letting dwellinghouse being used for short-term letting must have planning permission in order to be granted a short-term let licence.

4.17 The control area came into effect on 5 September 2022. This designation is likely to prove very controversial. Those in the sector will argue that the designation of the whole local authority area is disproportionate (taking a sledgehammer to crack a nut). Proponents of the control area may argue that designating only a part of the city would simply have pushed the issue of secondary short-term lets away from the city centre and into the suburbs. Certainly, the Council is very clear on what it is seeking to achieve:

This is the news we have been waiting for after years of leading the way in campaigning for change. I am delighted that Ministers have now, finally, answered our calls... For far too long, too many homes have been lost in our city to the holiday market. In fact, around a third of all short-term lets in Scotland are here in the Capital, so their associated issues of safety, anti-social behaviour and noise have a detrimental effect on many of our residents...This change to policy will help us to control the number of properties being unsuitably used in this way and help us to better balance housing supply for local people all year round, without stopping people from renting our rooms to performers during the festivals[37]. (Council Leader, Cammy Day)

4.18 At the time of writing (December 2022), the Council was consulting on its proposed changes to its non-statutory *Guidance for Business* with respect to short-term lets. It is not intended in this book to address that consultation in detail, but instead to set out what impact those changes might have. The background context to the consultation can be found in the Proposed Changes to Short-term Let Guidance report to Planning Committee dated 31 August 2022[38].

4.19 To date, the *Guidance for Business* has only given an indication of factors that the Council would take into account when deciding whether there had been a material change of use from residential to short-term letting. With the introduction of the Council's Short-Term Let Control Area, the Council has proposed changes

---

[37] Edinburgh to become first short-term let control area in Scotland – The City of Edinburgh Council

[38] 7.4 – Proposed Changes to Short-Term Let Guidance.pdf (edinburgh.gov.uk)

to its *Guidance* and has set out criteria which it would apply when considering Planning Applications for short-term letting.

4.20 The existing planning guidance sets out the following guidance in relation to short-term commercial visitor accommodation. The guidance does not set out how each of the bullet points will be assessed.

> *The change of use from a residential property to short-term commercial visitor accommodation may require planning permission. In deciding whether this is the case, regard will be had to:*
>
> - *The character of the new use and of the wider area;*
>
> - *The size of the property;*
>
> - *The pattern of activity associated with the use including numbers of occupants, the period of use, issues of noise, disturbance and parking demand; and*
>
> - *The nature and character of any services provided.*

4.21 The report to the Planning Committee dated 31 August 2022 proposed deleting that text, and replacing it with the following:

> *The city-wide Edinburgh Short-term Let (STL) Control Area came into force on 5 September 2022, which means that the use of a residential property for short-term commercial visitor accommodation will constitute a change of use requiring planning permission provided that:*
>
> - *It is not a private tenancy under Section 1 of the Private Housing (Tenancies) (Scotland) Act 2016;*

- *It is not a tenancy of a dwellinghouse (or part of one) where all or part of the dwellinghouse is the principal home of the landlord or occupier;*

- *Sleeping accommodation is provided to one or more persons for one or more nights for commercial consideration (i.e. an exchange of money);*

- *No person to whom sleeping accommodation is provided is an immediate family member of the person by whom the accommodation is being provided;*

- *The accommodation is not provided for the principal purpose of facilitating the provision of work or services to the person by whom the accommodation is being provided or to another member of that person's household;*

- *The accommodation is not provided by an employer to an employee in terms of a contract of employment for the better performance of the employee's duties; and*

- *The accommodation is not a hotel, boarding house, guest house, hostel, residential accommodation where care is provided to people in need of care, hospital or nursing home, residential school, college or training centre, secure residential accommodation (including a prison, young offenders institution, detention centre, secure training centre, custody centre, short-term holding centre, secure hospital, secure local authority accommodation or use as military barracks), a refuge, student accommodation or an aparthotel.*

These legal requirements are set out in the Town and Country Planning (Scotland) Act 1997 and the Town and Country Planning (Short-term Let Control Areas) (Scotland) Regulations 2021. Further detail is contained in Annex B of the Scottish

> *Government's Planning Circular 1 of 2021 – Establishing a Short-term Let Control Area.*
>
> *On 1 October 2022, the licensing scheme under the Civic Government (Scotland) Act 1982 (Licensing of Short-term Lets) Order 2022 (the STL Licensing Order) will open to receive applications for short-term let licences. The requirement to have an STL licence is separate from any need to have planning permission.*
>
> *In Edinburgh due to the STL Control Area, to lawfully operate a secondary let STL under an STL licence, there will be a need to either have planning permission in place, or an ongoing application for planning permission, or have it in place confirmation from the Council that planning permission is not required. In the event that the planning application and any related appeal is refused, the STL licence-holder cannot lawfully continue to operate the secondary let STL in terms of their licence.*

4.22   The Council's intention is to provide guidance as to how the Planning service will assess and determine short-term let licence applications against published criteria. There are two unknowns at the time of writing –(i) what criteria will come into effect following the Council's consultation on its revised *Guidance for Business* and (ii) what impact National Planning Framework 4 will have on the discussion. However, if criteria are adopted that is broadly along the lines of what is set out in the report to the Planning Committee, it will not be without difficulty (and potentially legal challenge). Some issues that will likely arise:

- When determining the character of the use, what is meant when it is said that consideration will be given to "where the location is mixed in character" such that there will be a presumption against planning permission? No definition is provided as to what is meant by "mixed in character".

- Why should it be that if a property is accessed off a stair where there are other flats off that stair it is very unlikely that a change of use will be supported? It is often argued that existing residents of flats within stairs are particularly affected by the pattern of activity which often results from short-term lets However, no evidence is provided in the Planning Committee report that would appear to justify the presumption against any change of use.

- Why should it be that a property with a communal garden is unlikely to be supported in terms of the planning permission application?

4.23 It will be interesting to see what type of responses there are to the consultation, whether the points mentioned above (or others) feature heavily in any responses, what criteria will be adopted by the local authority, and whether those criteria are legally justifiable.

Highland Council – short-term let control area

4.24 At the time of writing, only two local authorities had proceeded to implement a proposed short-term let control area – Edinburgh and Highland Council. Whilst Edinburgh Council has already given formal notice of its control area designation, Highland Council is not far behind – its proposed designation has been approved by Scottish Ministers and it is to be expected that notice will be given of the designation early in 2023.

4.25 At the Highland Council meeting on 9 September 2021, it was agreed that the Council would pursue the consideration of establishing a Short-term Let Control Area for Badenoch and Strathspey (also known as/referred to as Ward 20). Detailed consideration was undertaken at the Economy and Infrastructure Committee (EIC) meeting on 2 December 2021. Analysis has focused on the issues secondary letting is said to be having across Badenoch and Strathspey.

4.26   A public consultation lasting 6 weeks then followed, to which 332 representations were received. A report was presented to the Council on 30 June 2022[39], detailing the short-term let licensing regime and in respect of establishing a short-term let control area for Ward 20. It was agreed that the Council would progress with the establishment of a Short-term Let Control Area in respect of Badenoch and Strathspey. The Statement of Reasons, said to provide the information justifying the control area, as well as providing clarity on the boundary area for a Badenoch and Strathspey control area is available online[40].

4.27   It is certainly the case that some doubt existed as to the case for designating a control area. That doubt arose from the fact the Council's own officers appeared to have had misgivings when reporting on the available evidence said to justify the promotion of a control area in the report to the Economy and Infrastructure Committee on 2 December 2021[41].

4.28   It was accepted that the data "could not be considered to be entirely accurate or robust"[42], that "the available data does not conclusively demonstrate the number of properties being utilised solely as STL"[43], and that one option presented to the Committee was that the Committee agrees "that currently this number does not create undue amenity issues, unduly affect the housing supply or has a detrimental impact on local services and shops and does not warrant the establishment of a 'Control Area' across Ward 20"[44]. A second option was to postpone a decision on promoting

---

[39] Highland Council | The Highland Council

[40] Short-term Let Control Area | Badenoch and Strathspey Short-term Let Control Area – Statement of Reasons (highland.gov.uk)

[41] Economy and Infrastructure Committee | The Highland Council

[42] Para 6.5

[43] Para 6.24

[44] Para 6.25

THE INTERACTION BETWEEN PLANNING LAW AND LICENSING LAW

the Control Area "to allow more accurate data on the number and spread of STL across Ward 20 ....to be compiled..."[45].

4.29 Despite those apparent vulnerabilities in the underlying evidence base, the designation was nevertheless presented to the Scottish Ministers, and the proposed designation was recently approved by the Scottish Ministers in December 2022. On the basis that Highland Council will now proceed with the formalities of giving notice of the control area, it will be interesting to see what guidance (if any) is published by the local authority as regards the new control area.

Planning permission under the 2022 Order

4.30 Even if your property is not in a control area you may still need planning permission if there has been a material change of use to short-term letting in the last 10 years. It is important to be aware that changing the use of a dwellinghouse to provide short-term lets may constitute a material change of use requiring planning permission. Whether or not this is the case will depend upon the circumstances and factors which apply to the particular change of use.

4.31 The 2022 Order introduces two mechanisms by which the licensing authority may bring planning considerations into play during the licence application process – depending on whether the issue arises in the context of an existing host making an application prior to 1 April 2023[46], or in the context of a new host making an application (which would include an existing host who has made an application after 1 April 2023)[47]. It should be noted that as a consequence of the Scottish Government's decision to extend the deadline by which existing hosts need to

---

[45] Para 6.26
[46] Article 7 of the 2022 Order
[47] Paragraph 8 to Schedule 2 of the 2022

apply for a licence (in order to continue operating as a host pending determination of that application) by six months **to 30 September 2023**, and on the assumption that legislative approval is obtained in January 2023, it is expected that the reference to 1 April 2023 (in the context of these planning provisions) will be amended to 1 October 2023.

Existing hosts making an application prior to 1 October 2023

4.32   As we discussed in Chapter 3, there are certain transitional provisions in play that are designed to make the transition from unregulated host to licence-holder that bit easier for an existing host. Provided the existing host makes an application before 1 October 2023, the existing host can continue to take bookings and receive guests during the period the application is under consideration (including any subsequent appeal there may need to be to the Sheriff Court if the licence application is refused).

4.33   Even although the premises may not be in a control area, planning considerations remain a live issue. If the licensing authority considers that use of the premises for a short-term let would constitute a breach of planning control[48], then the licensing authority may, as soon as reasonably practicable after receipt of the application, notify the existing host/applicant that[49]:

- the licensing authority will suspend their consideration of the application for a period of **three months** beginning on the date of the notice,

- the existing host/applicant must, within that three-month period, submit (a) an application for planning permission

---

[48] In legal speak, that means a breach of planning control for the purposes of the Town and Country Planning (Scotland) Act 1997 by virtue of section 123(1)(a) or (b) of that Act

[49] Article 7(3) to 7(7) of the 2022 Order

or (b) apply for a certificate of lawfulness of use or development which would, if granted, remedy the considered breach, and

- the existing host/application must then notify the licensing authority that such an application for planning permission or certificate of lawfulness of use or development has been made.

4.34 This introduces a three-month grace period by which the existing host must make an application for planning permission or the necessary certificate. If the existing host does not take heed of this warning by the licensing authority, or the existing host has applied but the planning authority has refused the application for planning permission or a certificate (and no appeal is taken against that decision of the planning authority), then the local authority can refuse to consider the application for a short-term let licence. In short, the game is up!

Preliminary refusal: breach of planning control (for new hosts)

4.35 The 2022 Order has introduced a new ground upon which a licensing authority, when carrying out its consideration of an application for a short-term let licence in accordance with the 1982 Act, may decide to refuse to consider a licensing application for reasons relating to planning[50]. This will be known as a preliminary refusal. This is not the same as a licensing authority refusing to grant a licence application on its merits.

4.36 This is a largely discretionary decision to be taken by a local authority on a case-by-case basis. It is a power that will likely assist licensing authorities when dealing with applications for secondary letting in control areas. It does not apply to applications by existing hosts who make an application before 1

---

[50] Paragraph 8 to Schedule 2 of the 2022 Order, which inserts a new paragraph 2A to Schedule 1 of the 1982 Act

October 2023 (since those applications will be dealt with in the manner described in the section above). It will apply to applications by new hosts, and to applications by existing hosts but who miss the 30 September 2023 deadline. What will this look like in practice? Certain timescales must be adhered to:

1. **Within 21 days of the licensing authority having received an application for a licence**, the authority is entitled to refuse to consider the application (i.e. refuse to progress the application through to a final determination) when it considers that use of the premises for a short-term let would constitute a breach of planning control[51] (and it is worth noting that some licensing authorities, as part of their licensing policies, have indicated than an application will not be accepted or processed if it is not accompanied by planning permission or a certificate of lawfulness of use).

2. **Within 7 days of the licensing authority having refused to consider an application,** the authority must serve notice of that decision on (a) the applicant, (b) the relevant planning authority, and (c) the chief constable. That notice must include details of the licensing authority's reason for refusing to consider the application.

4.37 Provided those legislative requirements are met, the licence application will be brought to a halt by these preliminary refusal provisions.

4.38 That is not to say an applicant for a licence must return to the drawing board. There is a final way by which the licence application can be kept alive (and, perhaps more importantly, no further licensing fee needs to be paid). If a further application for a short-term let licence in relation to the same premises is made **within 28 days of the applicant subsequently obtaining** (a)

---

[51] For the purposes of the Town and Country Planning (Scotland) Act 1997 by virtue of section 123(1)(a) or (b) of that Act

planning permission or (b) a certificate of lawfulness of use or development, then the licensing authority is not permitted to levy a further licensing fee in respect of that further application.

Practical Considerations

Further planning guidance

4.39   In its planning circular published on 25 June 2021[52], the Scottish Government has issued guidance as to the material planning considerations that will be taken into account by a planning authority when determining whether or not to grant planning permission. For example:

- Whether guests have access to communal stairwells and gardens;

- The arrival and departure times of guests (particularly if these are at unsociable hours);

- Any reduction in the physical security of a building;

- The likely frequency and intensity of noise or anti-social behaviour;

- The number of guests staying;

- Impact on public services and residents' amenity; and

- The cumulative impact on public services and the character and amenity of a neighbourhood.

---

[52] Supporting documents – Planning circular 01/2021: short-term let control areas – gov.scot (www.gov.scot)

City of Edinburgh Council – licensing policy – rebuttable presumption against secondary letting

4.40 Although this chapter is principally about planning considerations, there is a very important aspect of the Edinburgh *licensing policy* that deserves consideration when discussing *planning* issues. That is because the short-term let licensing policy provides as follows:

> *For the purposes of this policy, secondary letting in tenement or shared main door accommodation is considered as unsuitable and there will be a rebuttable presumption, as defined in paragraph 2.9 of this policy, against the grant of a licence in such circumstances*[53].

4.41 This policy has been introduced because it is stated:

> *The Council has consistently called for the regulation of the STL sector through the introduction of a licensing scheme, as noted here. The Council believes that tenemental accommodation, or those with a shared main door, are unsuitable for secondary STL due to their character, location and risk of creating undue nuisance. The Council also has concerns in relation to the risk that anti-social behaviour may be exacerbated within tenement or shared main door accommodation given the close proximity of other residential accommodation and communal areas*[54].

4.42 It is more than arguable that this is a planning policy dressed up as being a licensing policy. If that is correct, then it is *ultra vires* (or unlawful) for the licensing authority to attempt to impose planning considerations into a licensing policy. Certainly, this rebuttable presumption appears to have little to do with safety

---

[53] Paragraph 4.14, City of Edinburgh Council Short-term Lets Licensing Policy

[54] Ibid, paragraph 4.13

concerns (which is what the new licensing scheme is intended to address) and everything about planning considerations.

4.43   Even if the licensing policy is able to avoid or resist a legal challenge, it will be essential that the licensing authority does not allow itself to essentially introduce a *de facto* ban on secondary letting within tenement or shared main door accommodation. It is a key principle that decision-makers (such as licensing committees) do not close their minds to the facts and merits of applications before them (in effect, to fetter their discretion) and do in fact engage with the exceptions that the licensing authority has identified as potentially overcoming the rebuttable presumption:

> *The Council may take certain factors into account when determining whether an application for secondary letting in tenement or shared main door accommodation be granted as an exception to its policy. Factors which may be considered include, but are not limited to the evidence of the following:*
>
> - *Neighbours consent/support*
>
> - *Length of time previously operated*
>
> - *Frequency of bookings or intensity of use of accommodation*
>
> - *System to prevent neighbour concerns*
>
> - *Low level of complaints*[55].

4.44   It will remain to be seen precisely how applications seeking to overcome the rebuttable presumption are treated by the committee.

---

[55] Ibid, paragraph 4.15

Glasgow City Council – planning policy

4.45   Glasgow City Council presently does not have any short-term let control areas. So, an application for short-term let application will require to be assessed against existing planning policy. In that sense, Glasgow City Council has a published planning policy that applies to, amongst other things, short-stay accommodation[56]. This is not a new issue – the planning policy has been in existence since at least 2017, and concerns matters that ought to have been complied with before now.

4.46   The key section is *4B: Short-Stay Accommodation*, as set out in paragraphs 4.10 to 4.16. Without going into the policy in unnecessary detail, it is possible to summarise the position as follows:

- in relation to *dwelling-houses*, the short-stay use of a house (whether or not it is the sole or principal resident of the occupants) is unlikely to require planning permission provided it is occupied as a single household;

- in relation to *flats*, occasional use as short-stay accommodation of an otherwise sole or main residence is unlikely to be a material change of use (a resident family renting a room to one lodger);

- where a *flat* is being used frequently to provide short-stay accommodation, there is *likely* to be a material change of use.

- The policy (at paragraph 4.16) refers to detailed criteria against which short-stay accommodation will be assessed.

4.47   It perhaps goes without saying that whilst a policy as regards the possible need for planning permission in respect of short-stay

---

[56]   CHttpHandler.ashx (glasgow.gov.uk)

accommodation exists, the policy itself is sufficiently flexible that it is not entirely conclusive as to when planning permission *is* required. Rather, it is easier to say when planning permission *is not* required.

4.48   Glasgow City Council's statement of licensing policy for short-term lets continues that theme. Paragraph 9.1 of the short-term let licensing policy sets out the discussion on whether or not planning permission might be required. For the reasons discussed above, it is not quite correct to say (as the licensing policy does) that "all flats require planning permission". The position is a little more nuanced than that.

4.49   However, what can be said is that the licensing policy is quite clear as to when an applicant would not require planning permission when applying for a short-term let licence:

- Home sharing whether the premises is a flat or a house;

- Secondary letting where the premises is a house;

- Home letting where the premises is a house.

Perth and Kinross Council – planning "checklist"

4.50   Whilst the majority of licensing authorities have referred to preliminary refusals in their published licensing policies in fairly broad terms, **Perth and Kinross Council** has published a checklist which is intended to assist potential applicants ascertain whether or not planning permission is required (although one could query why planning considerations such as external hot tubs, or external living areas, or outdoor communal areas have somehow worked their way into a licensing policy – this is yet another example of the line between licensing and planning law being blurred – if not exceeded – during the publication of short-term let licensing policies). It is said that if the answer is "yes" to any question then planning permission is deemed to be required…:

(a) Is your property a flat?

(b) Do any of your guests have to access the property via any communal areas? (i.e. shared gardens, stairwells, etc.)

(c) Does your property share a communal parking area? (i.e. it does not have its own designated space)

(d) Will any of your guests be regularly checking in or out at unsociable hours? (between 9pm and before 7am)

(e) Does your property have an external hot tub, an external living area (or similar), for use by guests in a predominately residential area?

(f) Do you allow parties to be held in the property by guests? (including accepting stag and hen bookings etc)

(g) Will the use of your property as a short-term let impact security for neighbours? (i.e. the use of key boxes for access and shared areas, such as entranceways or gardens)

(h) Have you changed any public rooms into additional accommodation? (ie changing a living room to a bedroom)

(i) Do you consider that the use of the property might detract from the character or amenity of the area in any way?

It therefore remains to be seen whether other licensing authorities will follow suit in publishing prescribed "checklists" for planning permission issues.

What if a short-term let control area is <u>subsequently</u> introduced in my local authority area?

4.51   Control areas should not be looked at in isolation as at the date a licence is applied for or granted. Rather, for the holder of a short-term let licence, it is an ongoing consideration. If a host obtains a licence for premises that are in an area subsequently designated

THE INTERACTION BETWEEN PLANNING LAW AND LICENSING LAW

as a control area, it is imperative to recognise that, whilst planning permission was not required at the application stage, it will almost certainly become relevant during the currency of the licence.

4.52 For licence-holders, it is a mandatory condition of a short-term let licence (in terms of the 2022 Order – mandatory conditions are discussed in Chapter 5) that if premises fall within a control area the licence-holder must ensure that planning permission requirements under the 1997 Act are complied with[57]. So, even though planning permission was not a mandatory requirement (nor did the local authority consider that planning permission was otherwise required) at the time the licence was applied for, the subsequent designation of a control area would mean the host would need to apply (in a timely manner) for either planning permission or a certificate of lawfulness of use.

4.53 Continuing to operate a short-term let without planning permission or a certificate, or after the refusal of planning permission or a certificate, would be a breach of one of the mandatory conditions of the short-term let licence. Serious consequences could then follow – see Chapter 8.

---

[57] Paragraph 13 to Schedule 3 of the 2022 Order

CHAPTER FIVE

THE MANDATORY CONDITIONS (AND ADDITIONAL CONDITIONS)

Introduction

5.1 Before turning to the detail of what the licence application process will look like, it is worth briefly considering what is meant by the mandatory conditions. These are licence conditions, introduced by Article 6 and Schedule 3 to the 2022 Order, which will apply to *all* types of short-term let licences all across Scotland. Whilst principally matters of concern for hosts and operators, as we will see there are certainly mandatory conditions that **booking platforms** and **other agencies** will want to be aware of in order to ensure the platforms play a role in hosts and operators being compliant with the new regime.

5.2 The mandatory conditions have ongoing effect. Put another way, it is not enough for an applicant to demonstrate, at the time of applying for a licence, that the applicant can/will comply with the mandatory conditions. For so long as the licence-holder has a short-term let licence, the mandatory conditions (and any additional conditions that might be applied by each local authority) must be complied with. Failure to comply with the mandatory (and additional) conditions would be a breach of the 2022 Order. That could lead to the short-term licence being revoked by the licensing authority, or could result in a criminal conviction and fine.

5.3 For operators who have been operating short-term lets before the legislation was introduced, or may have been renting out a property on a landlord/tenant basis, a number of these mandatory conditions concern safety issues that should have already been addressed (for example, fire safety and water safety). Whilst the mandatory conditions may sound like a significant regulatory burden (and they are), there is one mandatory condition that will be a relief for hosts and operators (and booking platforms). The 2022 Order has made clear that the mandatory conditions *must not impose a limit on the number of nights* for which premises may be used for *secondary letting*[58].

The mandatory conditions and practical considerations

5.4 Some of the mandatory conditions are self-evident in their effect, whereas there are other mandatory conditions worth commenting on.

Agents: Only those named as a holder of the licence can carry out the day-to-day management of the short-term let of the premises.

5.5 This is a slightly unusual mandatory condition. It may not even be practically achievable. In other forms of civic licensing, the reason why you might have a day-to-day manager listed on the licence application is because the licence-holder is a partnership or corporate entity and so would not necessarily have a "day-to-day" presence. By appointing or nominating a day-to-day manager or agent, there was a person who licensing officers and enforcement agencies could contact (especially in an emergency).

5.6 What I have described above is also consistent with what is set out in Part 1 of the Scottish Government Guidance: *Where you intend to appoint somebody else to manage your property, similar* [application] *details must be provided for your agent or day-to-day*

---

[58] Paragraph 2 to Schedule 2 of the 2022 Order

THE MANDATORY CONDITIONS (AND ADDITIONAL CONDITIONS)

manager, irrespective of whether you are applying as an individual or a corporate entity.[59]

5.7 It is not immediately obvious how both paragraph 2.13 of the Guidance and this mandatory condition are easily reconcilable. Indeed, the Scottish Government policy note (in describing details that licensing authorities must maintain on the public register) explains that the licensing authority must require contact details for the manager of the premises to be provided in circumstances **where the manager is different from the applicant**[60]. It will be interesting to see how licensing officers and committees interpret this mandatory condition, and whether a more flexible interpretation is given to the mandatory condition (for example, an employee of the corporate entity holding the licence carries out day-to-day management).

Type of Licence: The holder of the licence may only offer the type of short-term let for which the licence has been granted.

5.8 This is a clear statement that a licence-holder can only offer short-term lets of the type stipulated by the licence. For example, a host who applied for (and had granted) a home-letting or home-sharing licence would not be able to use that licence in order to undertake a secondary letting activity (or vice versa).

Fire Safety: the premises: The holder of the licence must ensure the premises has satisfactory equipment installed for detecting, and for giving warning of— fire or suspected fire, and the presence of carbon monoxide in a concentration that is hazardous to health.

5.9 The short point here is that all hosts and operators should ensure there are working smoke and carbon monoxide alarms. Hosts and operators should also be aware that the mandatory condition

---

[59] Paragraph 2.13, Part 1 of Guidance

[60] Paragraph 107, Policy Note, The Civic Government (Scotland) Act 1982 (Licensing of Short-term Lets) Order 2022, November 2021

should not be viewed as the bare minimum in terms of fire safety. It will be necessary for all licence-holders to comply with the Fire (Scotland) Act 2005. Licence holders will need to assess the risk of fire in the premises, identify and implement fire safety measures, and then keep those assessments and safety measures under review. Specialist advice should be sought if there is any doubt as to whether the premises comply with the Fire (Scotland) Act 2005.

Fire Safety: furniture and fittings: *The holder of the licence must keep records showing that all upholstered furnishings and mattresses within the parts of the premises which are for guest use, or to which the guests are otherwise permitted to have access, comply with the Furniture and Furnishings (Fire Safety) Regulations 1988.*

5.10   The 1988 Regulations impose certain requirements in relation to new domestic furniture such that the furniture will pass tests that the material used is not readily ignitable (for example, from cigarettes or matches). That includes labels being attached to furniture confirming certain information.

5.11   What might "records" look like? Photographic evidence of the furniture and its labels would be one option. Or perhaps even removing and retaining the labels. This is the sort of information that should be kept in your folder of key documents relating to your short-term let.

5.12   It is worth also observing that the mandatory condition only applies to **the parts of the premises which are for guest use or to which the guests are permitted to have access** (this is also the case for electrical safety). So, for home-sharing, where you may be letting out a spare room, the mandatory condition does not apply to furniture in rooms to which the guest does not/cannot have access. This might also arise in the context of secondary letting when there is a locked room to which the guest has no access.

Gas Safety: *Where the premises has a gas supply— (a) the holder of the licence*

THE MANDATORY CONDITIONS (AND ADDITIONAL CONDITIONS)

must arrange for an annual gas safety inspection of all gas pipes, flues and appliances in the premises, (b) if, after an annual inspection, any appliance does not meet the required safety standard, the holder of the licence must not allow a short-term let of the premises until the works necessary to bring the appliance to the required safety standard have been carried out.

Electrical Safety: *Where there are electrical fittings or items within the parts of the premises which are for guest use, or to which the guests are permitted to have access, the holder of the licence must—*

- *(a) ensure that any electrical fittings and items are in—*
  - *(i) a reasonable state of repair, and*
  - *(ii) proper and safe working order,*
- *(b) arrange for an electrical safety inspection to be carried out by a competent person at least every five years or more frequently if directed by the competent person,*
- *(c) ensure that, following an electrical safety inspection, the competent person produces an Electrical Installation Condition Report on any fixed installations,*
- *(d) arrange for a competent person to—*
  - *(i) produce a Portable Appliance Testing Report on moveable appliances to which a guest has access, and*
  - *(ii) date label and sign all moveable appliances which have been inspected.*

In determining who is competent, the holder of the licence must have regard to guidance issued by the Scottish Ministers under section 19B(4) of the Housing (Scotland) Act 2006.

5.13   It is convenient to comment on gas safety and electrical safety together. It is to be expected that all of the licensing authorities will, at the time of an applicant submitting an application, require confirmation that a gas safety check has been completed, as well as require confirmation that an EIC Report and PAT Report have been produced. You should be prepared to provide copies of the relevant certificates and reports with your application. Plainly if your premises does not have a gas supply, then that mandatory condition is of no relevance.

5.14 It will be obvious from reading the mandatory conditions that different safety checks are valid for different periods. The gas safety check requires to be undertaken annually. The electrical safety inspection must take place every five years. A short-term let licence may be granted for one, three, five years (or such other period as a licensing authority may determine). It is therefore essential that a licence-holder keeps on top of the regulatory requirements that impact upon the mandatory conditions, and instructs the necessary safety checks to be carried out in a timely manner.

Water Safety: Where the premises are served by a private water supply, the licence-holder must comply with the requirements on the owners of private dwellings set out in the Water Intended for Human Consumption (Private Supplies) (Scotland) Regulations 2017.

5.15 This mandatory condition only comes in to play when the premises has a private water supply (in which case the licence-holder must ensure compliance with the 2017 Regulations referred to in the condition). If your premises is supplied with water from Scottish Water, then you do not need to take any further action.[61]

Water Safety: legionella: The holder of the licence must assess the risk from exposure to legionella within the premises, whether or not the premises are served by a private water supply.

---

[61] Paragraph 2.34, Part 1 of the Guidance

THE MANDATORY CONDITIONS (AND ADDITIONAL CONDITIONS)

5.16   Part 1 of the Guidance explains that a risk assessment can be carried out by the licence-holder without the requirement for professional input. That is because it is said *the risks from hot and cold water systems in most residential settings are generally considered to be low because water is used regularly and does not stagnate*. It is still necessary to be able to demonstrate compliance with the mandatory condition. Some licence-holders may carry out the risk assessment themselves, in which case it is essential to keep a written record of how you carried out that risk assessment. Alternatively, licence-holders may simply prefer the peace of mind that a water safety professional has carried out the risk assessment and provided a legionella risk assessment report.

Safety and Repair Standards: The holder of the licence must take all reasonable steps to ensure the premises are safe for residential use. Where the premises are subject to the requirements of Chapter 4 of Part 1 of the Housing (Scotland) Act 2006, the holder of the licence must ensure that the premises meet the repairing standard.

5.17   Given the stated purpose of the licensing scheme is to ensure basic safety standards are in place across all short-term lets operating in Scotland, this mandatory condition is not at all surprising. In short, premises must be safe. Local authority Environmental Health Officers may be able to offer helpful advice.

5.18   The mandatory condition also refers to the repairing standard as it applies to Chapter 4 of Part 1 of the Housing (Scotland) Act 2006. In layman's language, the 2006 Act refers to a tenancy of a house that is let for human habitation (unless certain exclusions apply – see section 12(1) of the 2006 Act for more details). However, most relevant is that sections 12(3) and 12(4) of the 2006 Act ensure that the legislative obligations apply to short-term lets – since section 12(3) is clear that a short-term let is a type of tenancy to which the legislation applies (with the terms landlord, let and tenant to be construed in a manner that makes sense in a short-term let situation).

5.19 What then of the "repairing standard"? That is set out in fuller detail in section 13 of the 2006 Act, but hosts and operators should know that a short-term let will meet the repairing standard provided (in summary) the property is wind and water tight and reasonably fit for human habitation; the structure and exterior of the house are in a reasonable state of repair and working order; the installations for water, gas, electricity, sanitation and heating are in reasonable repair and working order; and fixtures, fittings, appliances, and furniture are safe and in proper working order.

Maximum Occupancy: *The licence-holder must ensure that the number of guests residing on the premises does not exceed the number specified in the licence.*

5.20 This is an interesting, and important, mandatory condition. When an applicant makes an application for a short-term let licence, it will be necessary to state in that application what the maximum occupancy of the premises is (i.e. how many guests can be safely accommodated in the premises). Some licensing authorities may have a way in which that maximum capacity should be calculated (with reference to the number and size of living rooms and bedrooms).

5.21 It is important to realise that the occupancy capacity applied for, and that granted by the licensing authority, may not be the same number! It is for the licensing authority to consider the facts and circumstances of the application and determine the maximum occupancy capacity. That number will then be stated on the licence that is issued to the applicant.

5.22 Care must also be taken, on a local authority by local authority basis, as to how children are calculated, and the age below which a child will not count towards the occupancy of the premises. The majority of licensing authorities have followed the Scottish Government guidance in that licensing authorities have set the age limit for which children do not count towards occupancy capacity as 'under 10 years', which is in line with the reference to children in the context of housing within the Housing Act (Scotland) 1987. However, some licensing authorities (**Clackmannanshire Council, Comhairle nan Eilean Siar, Dundee City Council, East Lothian Council, Falkirk Council, Fife Council, Glasgow City Council, Inverclyde Council, Perth and Kinross Council, Shetland Islands Council, Stirling Council, The Highland Council, West Dunbartonshire Council and West Lothian Council**) have published policies (in draft or adopted policies) that only children under two years old will be excluded from the maximum occupancy capacity calculations. It is not at all clear why there is this divergence across local authorities, and so applicants should take care to familiarise themselves with the licensing policies that apply to the area within which premises are located.

5.23 Finally, as a practical point, given the mandatory condition is to *ensure that the number of guests residing on the premises does not exceed the number specified in the licence*, it would be more than prudent to specify on any online listing precisely what the maximum occupancy capacity is for the premises. That will go some way to avoid a scenario such as a family of four (with children older than 10 years) attempting to book a listing that only has a maximum occupancy of three. It will also ensure compliance with the mandatory condition as regards Listings (see below) in which any advert or listing must be consistent with the terms of the short-term let licence (which includes the maximum occupancy capacity).

Information to be displayed: The holder of the licence must make the following information available within the premises in a place where it is accessible to all guests—

    (a) *a certified copy of the licence and the licence conditions,*

    (b) *fire, gas and electrical safety information,*

(c) *details of how to summon the assistance of emergency services,*

(d) *a copy of the gas safety report,*

(e) *a copy of the Electrical Installation Condition Report, and*

(f) *a copy of the Portable Appliance Testing Report.*

5.24 It was mentioned earlier in this chapter that, when making an application for a short-term let licence, the licensing authority may wish to see copies of the relevant compliance certificates. Another reason for ensuring your paperwork is in order is that much of the information that needs to accompany a licence application also has to be readily available on the premises for use by guests.

5.25 A simple "welcome pack" containing the usual welcome information, details of local facilities and amenities, etc is all that is required here, and which should contain copies of the information, reports, and certificates mentioned above.

Planning Permission: where the premises is in a short-term let control area for the purposes of section 26B of the Town and Country Planning (Scotland) Act 1997, where the use of the premises for a short-term let requires planning permission under the 1997 Act, the holder of the licence must ensure that either—

(a) *an application has been made for planning permission under the 1997 Act and has not yet been determined, or*

(b) *planning permission under the 1997 Act is in force.*

5.26 The interaction of planning law and licensing law has been discussed extensively in Chapter 4. The point worth repeating here is that if a local authority introduces a short-term let control area (for dwellinghouses for secondary letting) *after* a short-term let licence is granted, it will be necessary for the licence-holder to take reasonable steps, as quickly as possible, to ensure that if

THE MANDATORY CONDITIONS (AND ADDITIONAL CONDITIONS)

planning permission is required, then it is applied for and granted. Failure to do so would be a breach of the mandatory condition, and could lead to the licence being revoked or the licence-holder being prosecuted. This mandatory condition does not apply to premises outside of a control area.

Listings: The holder of the licence must ensure that any listing or advert (whether electronic or otherwise) for the short-term let of the premises includes—

(a) the licence number, and

(b) a valid Energy Performance Certificate rating if an Energy Performance Certificate is required for the premises, in accordance with the Energy Performance of Buildings (Scotland) Regulations 2008.

The holder of the licence must ensure that any listing or advert (whether electronic or otherwise) for the short-term let of the premises is consistent with the terms of the short-term let licence.

5.27 This is another interesting mandatory condition. What is plain is that there is a clear obligation on the licence-holder to ensure that any listing or advert includes the licence number and the EPC rating, and that the listing or advert otherwise reflects the terms of the short-term let licence (for example, whether it is a secondary let, the correct maximum occupancy, etc).

5.28 However, whilst this is a clear obligation on the licence-holder, it introduces interesting considerations for *booking platforms*. The 2022 imposes no obligations on booking platforms, and so there can be no breach of the legislation by booking platforms. Indeed, Part 2 of the Scottish Government Guidance really goes no further than encouraging booking platforms to try to help with the implementation of the new licensing scheme, and encourage compliance (by licence-holders) with the wording and spirit of the new legislation. Equally, the booking platform will not want to be seen to be condoning short-term letting activity taking place complications such a short-term licence has – such as control area consequences, etc).

Additional Licence Conditions

5.33   Unfortunately, simply complying with the nationwide mandatory conditions is not the end of the matter. Each applicant or licence-holder will, prior to submitting an application, want to get hold of the short-term let licensing policy that applies to their local authority area and carefully scrutinise its terms! It is beyond the scope of this book to analyse each of the 32 local authority licensing policies.

5.34   As a general observation, it is a well-documented matter of concern for those operating in the short-term let sector that many of the licensing authorities have approached the notion of additional conditions with far too much enthusiasm. Specifically, that licensing authorities have taken the power that has been bestowed upon them (to introduce additional conditions) and have instead set conditions that go well beyond a licensing function – straying in to matters of planning law, or are at risk of simply restating matters that are governed by other legislation, or have only peripheral relevance to the activity of providing short-term letting, or impose requirements upon a host that are simply outwith the host's control. Licensing officers and licensing committees would do well to remember that licensing conditions should only be concerned with the licensable activity. It will not be at all surprising if a licensing policy was the subject of judicial review, or an individual decision by a licensing committee to apply additional conditions to a licence was the subject of appeal.

5.35   It also remains to be seen how these additional conditions are applied in practice. One purpose of the additional conditions was to allow licensing authorities to specify conditions that would allow licensing authorities to properly tackle local issues. As it is, a reasonable number of the licensing authorities have adopted broadly similar additional conditions, based heavily on the style additional conditions proposed by the Scottish Government[63]. There seems to have been very little effort to justify (with reference to data or other supporting information) why those additional conditions need to apply to a particular local authority area. And there has been little suggestion that the additional conditions will be applied in anything other than a blanket approach to short-term let licences (irrespective of specific facts and merits, or localised issues). Time will tell if that is the default position.

5.36 To illustrate the point being made, what follows is not intended to be a critique of the of the pros and cons of the various policies adopted (or drafted) by the local authorities. Rather, what follows is a selection of the types of additional conditions (but by no means an exhaustive list) that are being considered by local authorities in order to highlight the wide spectrum of conditions that a host might be at risk of having applied to any licence.

Conditions potentially caught by existing legislation

5.37 Several local authorities (for example, **Aberdeenshire Council, East Renfrewshire Council, East Ayrshire Council, The Highland Council and West Dunbartonshire Council**) have potentially fallen into the trap of seeking to impose additional conditions for circumstances that are otherwise catered for by existing legislation. On one view, the additional conditions do not therefore really add anything (and so may not be viewed as objectionable, since the licence-holder should otherwise be complying with legislation); on the other hand, if the conditions are largely redundant they should not be imposed by a licensing committee in the first place.

5.38 Taking **East Renfrewshire Council** as an example, additional conditions 1, 2 and 9 are arguably conditions that are already covered by the requirements of the 1982 Act, the 2022 Order,

---

[63] Section 5, Part 2 of the Guidance

5.43 East Ayrshire Council has additional conditions in relation to hot tubs, spa pools and whirlpool baths. Aberdeenshire Council, East Renfrewshire Council, Fife Council, South Ayrshire Council and The Highland Council each has an additional condition concerned with the provision of hot tubs. It is insightful, but of course by no means definitive, that Comhairle nan Eilean Siar discusses the issue at paragraph 10.2 of its own licensing policy: *The Comhairle considered applying some additional specific conditions and documentation relating to equipment and items some short-term lets provide (i.e. hot tubs/spa pools/water sport equipment) but operators already have obligations under health and safety legislation.* It is a point that is well made.

5.44 To make provision for these additional conditions is certainly a noble endeavour. However, the question that legitimately arises is this: what have these conditions got to do with the activity of short-term letting (bearing in mind that the 2022 Order defines short-term let as being the use of residential accommodation provided by a host in the course of business to a guest)? Whilst the Scottish Government's stated intention was to put in place this licensing scheme to ensure basic safety standards are in place across all short-term lets operating in Scotland[64], it would appear to be improper to introduce additional conditions under the guise of "guest safety" when those additional conditions have little to do with the short-term let (as such) and more to do with activities (rafting) that are not licensable activities.

Carpets

5.45 Condition 5 of Perth and Kinross Council's licensing policy is framed as follows: *The licence-holder must ensure that the bedrooms, living room and hallway in the premises are carpeted.* This seems a quite remarkable condition, appears disproportionate (especially in the absence of any noise complaints by neighbours), is unlikely to be the sort of

---

[64] Paragraph 1.9, Part 1 of the Guidance

requirement imposed in a traditional landlord/tenant scenario, and is going to be an additional (unnecessary?) cost imposed upon those in the activity of short-term letting.

5.46   Perth and Kinross Council is not alone in drafting, although it is only a minority of licensing authorities who have drafted, a licensing condition imposing a requirement for rooms in the premises to be carpeted (whether requiring a carpet or vinyl floor covering with quality underlay, and potentially only arising following on from investigations into noise complaints). For example, similar conditions have been proposed (either in respect of premises, flats, or secondary letting) by **Argyll and Bute Council, City of Edinburgh Council, Dundee City Council, East Ayrshire Council, East Renfrewshire Council, Inverclyde Council, Scottish Borders Council, South Ayrshire Council** and **West Dunbartonshire Council.** Perth and Kinross Council has also ploughed a lone furrow in prescribing a planning policy "checklist" – which is discussed in chapter 4.

Miscellaneous conditions: decks, speakers and window opening restrictors…

5.47   Concluding this chapter is a look at some miscellaneous (and unusual) conditions, which might appear to be unnecessarily prescriptive, but which are being insisted upon only by **Clackmannanshire Council and Inverclyde Council.** If a short-term let licence is held in these licensing authorities, it is advisable to be aware that additional conditions can apply in respect of: (i) a requirement to advise guests that as a condition of booking they must provide details of a named person over the age of 21 years; (ii) a requirement to prohibit noise making equipment such as decks and speakers; and (iii) a requirement to ensure that window opening restrictor locks are provided to all windows which can be opened!

temporary exemptions and temporary licences in limited circumstances. **Orkney Islands Council, South Ayrshire Council, South Lanarkshire Council, The Highland Council, and The Moray Council** will permit temporary licences but not temporary exemptions. **Comhairle nan Eilean Siar** will permit applications for temporary licences only when applied for alongside an application for a full licence.

6.4 All of the remaining local authorities have taken the decision not to consider temporary exemptions or temporary licences: **Aberdeen City Council, Aberdeenshire Council (although the policy document refers to permitting what is referred to as temporary consent), Dumfries and Galloway Council, East Ayrshire Council, East Dunbartonshire Council, East Lothian Council, East Renfrewshire Council, Falkirk Council, Glasgow City Council (noting temporary exemptions may be considered for national events), Inverclyde Council, Midlothian Council, North Ayrshire Council, North Lanarkshire Council, Scottish Borders Council, West Dunbartonshire Council (noting temporary exemptions may be considered for national events).**

Temporary Licences

6.5 A local authority may permit the possibility of temporary licences which, if granted, will permit you to take bookings and welcome guests for a restricted period of time of up to six weeks[65]. You will be given a temporary licence number if you are granted a temporary licence.

6.6 One advantage of applying for a temporary licence is that a number of the normal application processes do not apply – for example the provisions allowing for representations and objections to the application to be made (although Police Scotland and Scottish Fire and Rescue Service will still be

---

[65] Paragraph 7 of Schedule 1 to the 1982 Act

consulted), the need to display a site notice, notifying changes and alterations, variation of the licence, appeal provisions, etc.

6.7 A temporary licence is quite restrictive. If you have not applied for a full licence, your temporary licence can only run for a period of up to 6 weeks. Nor can a temporary licence be renewed. However, if you have also applied for an ordinary licence for the same premises and the same activity, then your temporary licence will continue to be valid until your full licence application is determined by the licensing committee (whether granted, refused, or the subject of a Sheriff Court appeal). For a temporary licence to be granted, your short-term let must comply with the mandatory conditions, including having planning permission in place if you are required to have it.

6.8 There is, however, a somewhat illogical approach being adopted by a significant number of local authorities who have taken the decision (as set out in their short-term licensing policies) not to permit **any** type of temporary licence. That approach is said to be because of limited consultation process, the issue of public/guest safety, and other statutory requirements. However, the same criticisms could be made of any temporary licence application made under the 1982 Act (and it is to be remembered that paragraph 7 to Schedule 1 of the 1982 Act expressly empowers licensing authorities to grant civic licences on a temporary basis). Many of those local authorities already permit temporary licences for other activities regulated by the 1982 Act, for example public entertainment licences, taxi booking office licences, and other civic licences.

6.9 When this is also viewed in the context that the licensing scheme was introduced in order to ensure basic safety standards for short-term lets, that the Scottish Government has legislated for the licensing of short-term lets, and the Scottish Government Guidance expressly anticipates that temporary licensing can apply to short-term lets, it seems difficult to justify a policy position of not granting temporary licences – apparently because the requirements of the 1982 Act are less strictly imposed, or for arguments apparently connected to safety standards.

6.10 If that seems illogical, matters are even more complex in **Edinburgh**. That is as a consequence of what is set out in paragraphs 4.17 to 4.30 of the authority's Licensing Policy, *which is essentially a prohibition on temporary licences for secondary letting*. What is not at all clear from Edinburgh's Licensing Policy, and which is not substantiated by any reasons, is why temporary licences may only be granted for home sharing and home letting (but not secondary letting). There is no explanation in the licensing policy as to why temporary licences are unsuitable for secondary letting.

Temporary Exemption

6.11 A temporary exemption affords the ability to take bookings and accept guests in a property without having a licence in place. During special events (for example, festivals, major sporting events, etc.), a licensing authority may grant a temporary exemption for a fixed period of time which allows a host to operate despite not having a licence.

6.12 There is a very interesting distinction between what the legislation says about temporary exemptions, and what interpretation the Scottish Government has insisted upon in its Guidance. In terms of the 2022 Order, a licensing authority may, on application made to it, grant an exemption from the requirement to obtain a short-term let licence in relation to a specified property or properties and **during a specified period (which must not exceed 6 weeks in any period of 12 months)**[66]. In terms of the Scottish Government Guidance, a licensing authority may grant an exemption from the requirement to

---

[66] Paragraph 6 of Schedule 2 to the 2022, introducing paragraph 1A to Schedule 1 of the 1982 Act

obtain a short-term let licence **for a specified single continuous period not exceeding 6 weeks in any period of 12 months**[67].

6.13 Emphasis has been deliberately added. There is a small but subtle difference between what the law says and what the Scottish Government has encouraged licensing authorities to apply in practice. Certainly, one reading of the 2022 Order would permit an applicant, for example, to first apply for a temporary exemption in relation to a specified property for a specified period (such as, 4 weeks) and thereafter make a second application for an exemption (within that period of 12 months) provided the cumulative total of the specified periods covered by any exemption does not exceed 6 weeks.

6.14 That would also be a logical approach, as it would allow those parts of the country where there is a strong summer season (whether that is for local festivals and international events) and an equally strong two-week period over the festive season to permit a host or operator to obtain a temporary exemption, taking advantage of both seasonal occasions. That would be particularly advantageous in meeting the increased demand for short-term tourist accommodation in those parts of the country. As it is, the Scottish Government interpretation as to how the six-week period in any 12-month should be enforced will require a host or operator to elect between the summer season or the winter season. That is, I think, to the detriment of the potential for the temporary exemption.

6.15 In order to be granted the exemption, it is still necessary to apply to the relevant licensing authority for a temporary exemption. This process will be slightly different to the licence (or temporary licence) application process, should take much less time to be granted, and ought to have a lower fee. In processing an application for a temporary exemption, the licensing authority may consult with Police Scotland and the Scottish Fire and

---

[67] Paragraph 1.17, Part 1 of the Guidance

Rescue Service. Although the exemption application process ought to be less time consuming, a successful applicant will still be required to comply with some of the mandatory conditions. These mandatory conditions include your property having planning permission where required, meeting a number of safety standards, and not exceeding a maximum occupancy level.

6.16 The 2022 Order is very clear that a licensing authority may elect not to grant any temporary exemptions, or may not grant temporary exemptions for certain types of premises[68] – all of which needs to be recorded in the licensing authority's short-term let licensing policy. As with temporary licences, several local authorities have resolved not to grant any temporary exemptions at all. Again, it is not clear how a licensing authority can resolve the apparent conflict between refusing to allow temporary exemptions for reasons of public/guest safety in circumstances where the Scottish Government (presumably having issues such as public safety in mind) expressly legislating for the principle of temporary exemptions.

---

[68] Paragraph 6 of Schedule 2 to the 2022, introducing paragraph 1A(4) to Schedule 1 of the 1982 Act

CHAPTER SEVEN

THE APPLICATION PROCESS

Introduction

7.1 I chose to deliberately order the book in this manner: you have worked out whether you are even in short-term let licence territory (Chapter 2); you have established whether you are new or existing host (and what that means for continued trading beyond 1 October 2023), and what type of licence is required (Chapter 3); you have started to familiarise yourself with the minefield that is planning law (Chapter 4); it has become apparent there are lots of mandatory conditions that are going to require proof (certificates, etc) of regulatory compliance (Chapter 5); and you have considered the question of whether a temporary licence (if that is your preferred option) is even possible for you in your local authority area (Chapter 6). All that is left is to make the application.

7.2 One of the benefits of the Scottish Government electing to bolt the new short-term licensing scheme onto the 1982 Act is that it means there is fairly well trodden path as to what the application process should look like. Seasoned veterans of the 1982 Act may find this chapter a little basic. However, it is still an important aspect of the new licensing scheme.

The relevant licensing authority

7.3 The first step will be to establish the local authority area in which the premises are situated. Since, having established that factual issue, everything else thereafter will flow from it. The licensing authority for that area will have published its licensing policy (and which is essential reading for anyone thinking of making an application, or applying on someone else's behalf), will have made available the necessary application forms, and will almost certainly have published online guidance for the making of an application for a short-term let licence.

7.4 Any application to a licensing authority for the grant or renewal of a licence will need to be in writing, be signed by the applicant or agent, and be accompanied by the necessary fee[69]. Almost without exception, the licensing authorities across Scotland have made clear that applications will not be processed if they are not submitted with all of the necessary accompanying documents and have had the relevant fee paid. Unfortunately, there is no statutory form of application for civic licences under the 1982 Act. Although it will be left to the discretion of the licensing authorities, it is to be expected that all of the licensing authorities will follow a broadly similar approach.

7.5 The question of fees has been a divisive and politically sensitive subject. The Scottish Government has been clear that the expectation is for licensing authorities to keep costs down through economies of scale, integrating service delivery with other licensing functions, and taking a proportionate approach to checks and verifications[70]. Such an expectation does not appear to have been borne out in practice.

7.6 There is no uniform, nationwide approach to the issue of fees (although that, of itself, is not particularly surprising). However, there is significant disparity across the local authority areas. For example, the position in the draft policy for **Falkirk Council** is relatively easy to follow. A home share or home let licence for up to four people will cost £125, and for five or more people will cost £250. For a secondary let licence, the cost is £250 and £400, respectively. Licensing authorities such as **Comhairle nan Eilean**

---

[69] Paragraph 1 to Schedule 1 of the 1982 Act.

[70] Para 3.3 of Part 2 of the Guidance.

THE APPLICATION PROCESS

Siar, **Glasgow City Council, East Ayrshire Council, North Ayrshire Council and South Ayrshire Council** apply a broadly similar feeing structure. Meanwhile, in **Shetland Islands Council** the maximum fee applied to any short-term let licence application is £208…!

7.7   The situation in other parts of the country is quite different. For example, **Aberdeen City Council** proposed a tiered structure of fees, starting at £420 where the guest capacity was 1-2 persons, and ranging through to an incredible £2,980. In **Edinburgh**, home sharing and home letting is a modest £120 for a new application, whilst for secondary letting the starting cost is £652 for an occupancy of 1-3 persons, increasing to £1,089 for 4-5 person, through to £5,669 for (albeit, in the unlikely event of) an occupancy of 21+ persons. One could also find fairly punitive fees for **Dundee City Council, Perth and Kinross Council**, and **Renfrewshire Council**.

7.8   In addition to the fee that will require to be paid along with the licensing application, it is important for hosts to be aware that the licensing authority may also impose fees upon licence-holders for the inspection of premises. Fees should not be charged for any inspection carried out as part of the application process or as part of ongoing monitoring, but fees may be levied by the licensing authority if an inspection is required because of a failure to comply with a licence condition or following a complaint relating to the premises (which is not vexatious or frivolous)[71]. Where such a fee issued, it is important to be aware that the licensing authority is obliged to produce a report of its findings to the licence-holder within 28 days of the inspection or refund the fee that was charged[72].

---

[71] Introduced by paragraph 15(1)(e) of Schedule 2 to the 2022 Order

[72] Introduced by paragraph 15(4) of Schedule 2 to the 2022 Order

7.9   It will also be necessary to establish what the licensing authority requires by way of accompanying certificates. It is expected that licensing authorities will operate a blend of self-declaration of certain matters and copy certificates for other matters (generally speaking, all of the matters covered by the mandatory conditions). For example, the licensing authority may be prepared to accept an applicant's self-declaration that a legionella risk assessment has been carried out and insurances are in place, but will expect to see copies of planning permission, EIC Reports, PAT reports, gas safety certificates, and layout plans of the premises.

Layout plans

7.10   Given short-term let licences are concerned with the use of premises, it is not surprising that licensing authorities require a layout plan (of sorts) to be submitted with the application. That is because the licensing authority needs to understand what sort of premises it is licensing, how big it is, what the maximum occupancy capacity can be, and so on.

7.11   What is more concerning is the lack of uniformity across Scotland to this issue. Many local authorities require a layout plan to be provided, but without being overly prescriptive as to the requirements for the layout plan. To use just four examples: **Angus Council** requires a layout plan and it would be "helpful" for the layout plan to describe the escape routes, location of heat/smoke alarms, the layout of rooms, etc. **Dundee City Council** requires a plan of the premises, preferably to a 1:50 scale. **East Ayrshire Council** requires a floor plan of the premises to be submitted on a scale of 1:100. Meanwhile, one takeaway point from the **Orkney Islands Council** licensing policy is the exacting requirements introduced as regards the preparation of those plans:

> *Applications for licences, including temporary licences, must therefore be accompanied by floor plans in accordance with the*

requirements below.

These should be provided electronically where possible, including via email.

Three (3) coloured printouts to scale must be provided when requested.

Floor plans must show the following:

- *the extent of the boundary of the building and the external and internal walls of the premises;*

- *the location and names of any streets surrounding the building from which guests have access to the premises;*

- *the location and width of each point of access to and egress from the premises;*

- *the location and width of any other escape routes from the premises;*

- *the location of any equipment used for the detection or warning of fire or smoke or for fighting fires;*

- *the location of any steps, stairs, elevators or lifts in the premises;*

- *any accommodation intended for guests with mobility impairment;*

- *the number of rooms intended for sleeping; and*

- *the maximum occupancy capacity of the building (excluding children under 10 years old).*

- *A floor plan may include a legend through which the matters narrated above may be sufficiently illustrated by the use of symbols on the plan.*

Floor plans should preferably be in the following format:

- *All applications: premises drawings, possibly professional prepared, at a scale of 1:100 and a location plan at a scale of 1:1250 or 1:2500 for rural locations.*

7.12   You might be forgiven for thinking the policy was in respect of an application for a premises licence under the Licensing (Scotland) Act 2005! It is unlikely that this was the policy intention when a short-term let licensing scheme was conceived. It is for the best that other local authorities have not followed the Orkney Islands Council's lead in setting out such detailed requirements for a plan to accompany a short-term let licence application, since such a policy position will only likely serve to deter would-be applicants from embarking on the licensing process!

Applicants

7.13   Having settled upon the correct local authority, the next step of the process is to establish who it is that is making the application.

7.14   Where the applicant is an individual, the 1982 Act requires details of the person's full name and address, address history for the last five years, email address, telephone number, date and place of birth, and details of any day-to-day manager. Where the applicant is a partnership, company, etc, the application form will require details of the registered/principal office, the names, addresses, dates and places of birth of its directors or partners, and details of the day-to-day manager[73]. That much is common ground for any civic licence under the 1982 Act.

---

[73] Paragraph 1 of Schedule 1 to the 1982 Act

Owner consent

7.15 The 2022 Order has introduced a further requirement, which arises if the applicant is not the owner of the premises concerned with the activity of short-term letting. Where the applicant is not the owner of the premises, or the land on which the premises are located (or shares ownership of the premises or the land), then the application form will need to disclose the name and address of the owner(s), and contain a declaration from the owner(s) that they consent to the application[74].

Day-to-day managers

7.16 The Guidance refers to day-to-day managers as any people that might be asked to carry out the day-to-day management of the accommodation[75]. That could be an employee of the applicant, or the applicant's letting agency (including details of the directors/partners of the letting agency). All of that said, the application form does not require an applicant to drill down to a granular level of details – cleaners employed to enter the premises for the purposes of their role/employment would not be considered to be involved in the day-to-day "management" of the accommodation.

Publicity

7.17 When an application is then made to a licensing authority, there are three key events that ensure the application process is truly underway.

7.18 The first is that the licensing authority (as soon as reasonably practicable after receiving an application) must issue a unique number to the applicant in the form of a **temporary licence**

---

[74] Paragraph 5 of Schedule 2 to the 2022 Order
[75] Paragraph 3.10 of Part 1 of the Guidance

number[76]. That will be important for existing hosts wishing to continue operating after 1 October 2023, and who may need to demonstrate to booking platforms and letting agents that they did in fact apply in a timely fashion in order to benefit from the transitional provisions made available to existing hosts.

7.19   The second is that a copy of the application will be sent to Police Scotland and to Scottish Fire and Rescue Service for comment[77].

7.20   The third is that the applicant must display a notice at or near the premises stating that an application has been made, providing certain statutory particulars, and providing information on how an objection or representation can be made by an interested party for the application. The site notice must be on display for 21 days beginning with the date on which the application was submitted to the licensing authority. The site notice must be positioned in such a way that it can be conveniently read by the public[78].

7.21   Once the 21-day period has expired, it is incumbent on the applicant to then complete and return a certificate to the licensing authority confirming that the site notice was on display, uninterrupted, for that 21-day period[79]. I have seen occasions when objectors have attempted to argue that the site notice was not in place at all, or had become dislodged at some point during the 21-day period. For that reason, it may be prudent for applicants to take time-stamped photographs of the site notice (it is not suggested that the notice should be photographed every day – the key point is having some sort of evidential reference point that the site notice was on display). If the notice was not displayed at all, or the applicant did not take reasonable steps for the

---

[76] Paragraph 2(1A) of Schedule 1 to the 1982 Act, introduced by the 2022 Order

[77] Paragraph 2(1) of Schedule 1 to the 1982 Act

[78] Paragraph 2(2) and 2(3) of Schedule 1 to the 1982 Act

[79] Paragraph 2(4) of Schedule 1 to the 1982 Act

protection or replacement of the notice, or the statutory certificate is not submitted, then the licensing authority may require the applicant to re-display the notice again for a further period of 21 days[80].

Objections and representations

7.22　It is a hard fact of licensing life that frequently applications for civic licences under the 1982 Act (and, indeed, under other licensing regimes) are objected to. This is not, however, a complete free for all, and certain statutory requirements must be met.

7.23　Importantly, an objection must (amongst other things) be in writing, must specify a ground of objection (these are usually linked to the statutory grounds of refusal; it cannot simply be a bald assertion without any explanation or justification), must contain the name and address of the objector (anonymous objections will not be tolerated), and must be made within 28 days of the date when the public notice was first displayed[81]. It is to be remembered, however, that the licensing authority does retain a discretion to entertain a late objection or representation if the authority is satisfied there is sufficient reason for the lateness[82] (and, indeed, the authority also retains a discretion to exclude entirely objections and representations that are obviously irrelevant).

7.24　It can, I think, be safely assumed given the local tensions that short-term lets can cause that we will see a reasonable number of neighbour objections being made to short-term let licences –

---

[80] Paragraph 2(6) of Schedule 1 to the 1982 Act
[81] Paragraph 3(1) of Schedule 1 to the 1982 Act
[82] Paragraph 3(2) of Schedule 1 to the 1982 Act

specifically, applications for a secondary let licence. Copies of any objection will, of course, be sent to the applicant[83].

Disposal of applications for grant and renewal of licence

7.25   As has already been discussed in Chapter 4, a licensing authority may suspend or refuse consideration of an application if the authority considers the use of the premises for a short-term let would constitute a breach of planning control[84].

7.26   Assuming an application is not caught up in arguments over planning permission, the application should proceed to consideration by the relevant licensing or regulatory committee. In many ways, the process is an inquisitorial one – the licensing authority is empowered to make such reasonable inquiries into an application as it sees fit[85]. Put another way, the licensing authority is not constrained in its decision making to only the material that might happen to be put before it – provided the applicant is notified. The committee members may even wish to visit the premises – either because they are unfamiliar with the layout of the premises or because they may wish to assess whether the premises can comply with the mandatory conditions.

7.27   Many – if not all – of the licensing authority policy statements have indicated an intention that provided an application is not objected to, it will be granted under delegated powers. What that means in practice is that the application will be granted administratively, without the need for a hearing. That much is good news for applicants who might be concerned about the rising costs of the application process (especially if a decision is taken to instruct a licensing practitioner to attend any hearing on the applicant's behalf).

---

[83] Paragraph 3(4) of Schedule 1 to the 1982 Act

[84] Article 7 and Paragraph 2A of Schedule 1 to the 1982 Act

[85] Paragraph 4(1) of Schedule 1 to the 1982 Act

7.28   However, where an application is in receipt of representations and objections, a hearing will almost certainly be convened (albeit the 1982 Act permits a licensing authority to proceed by way of written submissions[86]) at which the applicant will have an opportunity to argue the case for the grant of a licence[87] (and objectors will be given the opportunity to make their case in respect of any objection).

7.29   It is generally accepted that licensing hearings are intended to be heard expeditiously and disposed of without being bogged down too much by legal formality. There is no entitlement to insist upon the leading of evidence (in the traditional court room sense). The rules of evidence as might apply to a court hearing are largely absent from a licensing hearing. Applicants and objectors (or their representatives) will make submissions on the application and may rely on documentation in support of those submissions. The dividing line between relevant and irrelevant material is less clear, although a well-convened licensing committee (and a strong convenor) will ensure that objectors do not stray far from the terms of their objection and that no parties at the hearing trespass onto clearly irrelevant matters.

The licensing hearing[88]

7.30   A nerve-wracking occasion, especially for the uninitiated. Often held in grand looking council chambers, this is the opportunity for an applicant to make his or her case heard. The applicant may have a legal representative, or may be arguing the case on their own. Objectors may or may not be in attendance. The hearing will be chaired by the convenor of the relevant committee, and with other councillors appointed to sit on that committee in attendance. Also in attendance will be the statutory consultees –

---

[86] Paragraph 4(3) of Schedule 1 to the 1982 Act
[87] Paragraph 4(2) of Schedule 1 to the 1982 Act
[88] Paragraph 5 of Schedule 1 to the 1982 Act

certainly Police Scotland, who will often be flanked by licensing officers, as well as officers from other council departments (such as building standards and planning). The atmosphere will range from light-hearted (perhaps even jovial) to much more serious. Given the inquisitorial nature of proceedings, and the fact that traditional court rules as to evidence and procedure tend not to apply, the hearing has the risk of being a little unpredictable as to the questions that might crop up (and thus the direction of travel for the hearing).

7.31 In terms of order of procedure, the licensing committee will generally hear from the statutory consultees first, the applicant will be given an opportunity to state his or her case, and any objectors in attendance will get the opportunity to do likewise. There will likely be questions from the committee that require to be answered, before the applicant (or the applicant's representative) has an opportunity to sum up the application. Ultimately, the licensing committee requires to reach a decision, whether that is to grant or to refuse the application that is before it (with or without conditions being attached).

7.32 In granting or renewing an application, the committee will impose the mandatory conditions and apply any additional conditions that are thought fit. There is one exception as to the additional conditions that might be imposed – the 2022 Order is commendably clear that the Committee must not impose any limit on the number of nights for which premises may be used for secondary letting[89]. Beyond that exception, the Committee does have the discretion to impose such conditions as the Committee thinks may be necessary – but that is subject to the usual public law considerations (which are beyond the scope of this book) that the conditions are reasonable, lawful, sufficiently precise, and so on. As we discussed in Chapter 5, it should also be the case that additional conditions should only be concerned

---

[89] Paragraph 9 to Schedule 2 to the 2022 Order

with the licensable activity (as opposed to simply being considered desirable in a general sense). Whilst many of the licensing authorities have set out in their licensing policies a series of additional conditions that may be applied when a licence is granted, it is important that the licensing authority does not close its mind to the possibility that some or all of the additional conditions are to be disapplied in respect of a particular licence.

Grounds of refusal[90]

7.33 Whilst every application hopes to be granted or, at the minimum, granted with conditions attached (and there will be occasions when an applicant might feel as though they are presented with an invidious choice – either have the application granted with conditions that are less than desirable, or have the application refused), it is important to be aware of the *statutory* grounds for refusal.

7.34 I emphasise the word statutory, since a licensing committee does not have a free hand to simply refuse an application for whatever reason it might choose – the 1982 Act prescribes the basis upon which an application may be refused. That said, as will be seen below, the statutory grounds of refusal are worded in a way that allows a licensing committee to retain a degree of flexibility to its decision-making (provided, of course, that the licensing committee has before it – whether as part of the application, or as a result of an objection or representation, or as a consequence of the committee's own inquiries – material that would permit the committee to lawfully and reasonably reach such a conclusion).

7.35 A licence may be refused because the licensing committee considers:-

---

[90] Paragraph 5(3) to Schedule 1 to the 1982 Act

(a) the applicant or, in the case of a company/partnership, etc any director of it or partner in it or any other person responsible for its management, is either disqualified under section 7(6) of the 1982 Act, or is not a fit and proper person to be the holder of the licence.

It is for the licensing committee to determine that a person is not a fit and proper person to be the holder of a licence (as opposed to the applicant having to prove he or she is a fit and proper person – although, if criticisms are made in respect of the applicant's conduct or character then it is for the applicant to provide the committee with his or her explanation rather than simply ignore such adverse comments).

The Scottish Government Guidance sets out examples of the types of matters licensing committees are likely to take into account[91], such as (a) criminal convictions or other relevant non-conviction information that may be supplied by Police Scotland (it is for the licensing committee to assess the weight and relevance of those convictions and information as it applies to an assessment as to whether the applicant is fit and proper to hold a short-term let licence); (b) being disqualified from being a private landlord or having had letting agent or property factor registration revoked now or in the past; (c) having had a licence for short-term lets or House in Multiple Occupation revoked by a licensing authority; (d) having had an application for a short-term lets licence refused by any licensing authority; and (e) providing false or misleading information in an application for a short-term lets licence, HMO licence, or application to be a private landlord (lying to a licensing authority, or not providing the whole truth, will be conduct

---

[91] Paragraph 3.17 of Part 1 of the Guidance

that a licensing authority takes a negative view on and must be such as to render a person unfit to hold a licence).

(b) where the short-term let activity would be managed by or carried on for the benefit of a person, other than the applicant, who would be refused the grant or renewal of such a licence if he made the application himself.

If the licensing authority has material before it (whether allowing it to conclude as a matter of fact, or perhaps by inference) that the short-term let activity is being carried on for the benefit of a third party (in this case, the benefit is likely to be the financial benefit of the taking of short-term let bookings), then the application may be refused provided that one of the grounds of refusal applies to that third party person.

(c) the premises are not suitable or convenient for the conduct of short-term letting having regard to—

- the location, character or condition of the premises;
- the nature and extent of the proposed activity;
- the kind of persons likely to be in the premises;
- the possibility of undue public nuisance;
- public order or public safety.

Material that may justify this ground of refusal is likely to come to the licensing committee by virtue of an objector, the local authority licensing officers, or Police Scotland. Given the stated purpose in the Scottish Government guidance of this new licensing scheme is "to ensure basic safety standards are in place across all short-term lets operating in Scotland"[92] and to assist with handling complaints and address issues (public nuisance, public order, and public safety) faced by neighbours effectively, it is to be expected that the suitability of the premises for short-term letting will be an issue that is keenly scrutinised by licensing committees, in line with published licensing policies. Of course, as with any application for a civil licence, the licensing committee must still have before it sufficient factual material that allows it to form a conclusion that this ground of refusal may be relied upon.

(d) The applicant would not be able to secure compliance with the mandatory or additional licence conditions (or any further conditions to which the licence is to be subject), or the application does not contain the required consent of the owners of the premises[93]

(e) there is other good reason for refusing the application (which, frankly, is very wide in its terms and confers upon the committee a wide measure of discretion as to what is "other good reason").

7.36 An applicant should bear in mind that if the application is refused, that applicant is prohibited, **within one year**, from making an application for the grant of the same kind of licence in respect of the same short-term let activity consisting of or including the same use of the same premises unless in their opinion there has been, since their refusal, a material change of circumstance[94].

7.37 Two key points emerge from the statutory prohibition on "successive applications" within one year. The application would

---

[92] Para 1.9 of Part 1 of the Guidance
[93] Introduced by paragraph 9 of Schedule 2 to the 2022 Order
[94] Paragraph 6 of Schedule 1 to the 1982 Act

need to be made for the same short-term let activity. So, if an application had been refused in respect of premises for a secondary letting licence, the 1982 Act would not prevent an applicant reassessing matters and returning to the licensing committee within one year with an application for a home letting licence.

7.38   A material change of circumstances is not necessarily easy to define. But, the types of material change that might justify a renewed application within one year of a refusal could include any criticisms by the Police or Scottish Fire and Rescue Service (that led to the initial refusal) having been entirely remedied, or perhaps that the applicant can now demonstrate that all of the mandatory conditions as to electrical safety, fire safety, etc can now be complied with (when, at the time of the initial refusal, there were significant deficiencies in the application). In short, the applicant would want to demonstrate that issues in relation to the premises had been materially rectified or improved, in order to persuade the committee to entertain a further application within the one-year prohibition window.

Licence duration

7.39   All being well, the short-term let licence will be granted, whether that is under delegated powers or following appearance at a hearing of the licensing authority. A licence number will be issued. The format of the licence number will be common across all of Scotland. The Scottish Government has indicated that every licence number will comprise 8 characters in the format: 2 letters – 5 numbers – 1 letter[95]. The first two letters will denote the local authority area. The five numbers will be issued by each licensing authority. The final letter will denote the type of licence. Here, there are five options: E (temporary exemption); T (temporary licence); P (provisional licence number issued on

---

[95]   Annex A of Part 2 of the Guidance

receipt of licence application); F (First – full – licence); R (renewed licence).

7.40 What then of the licence duration? This is not as simple a topic as one might initially assume. The starting position is what the 1982 Act says. The maximum period for which a new licence can be granted is three years, but it is entirely open to the licensing committee to grant a new application for a period of less than three years[96]. Typically, the licensing committee's policy should set out the licence duration that will be granted for a home letting, home sharing, and secondary letting licence. That at least allows an applicant to have an understanding as to likely disposal. However, if a new application is particularly contentious, there are multiple objections, but the licensing committee is sufficiently persuaded as to the principle of granting a licence, it might only grant the licence for a period of one year in order to "test" how the short-term let activity is ultimately carried out.

7.41 I say the starting position is the 1982 Act. However, it is just as important to understand the various licensing authority policies on the question of duration – which are varied. On the one hand, **Edinburgh** is clear that a secondary letting application will only be granted for one year. Almost all of the other authorities will readily grant all types of short-term let licence for the full period of three years.

7.42 The question of renewal applications may seem like quite some time away (at the time of writing, some applications may have been applied for, but very few likely to have been granted). However, it is worth noting that provided a renewal application is made prior to the expiry of the existing licence, then the existing licence shall continue to have effect until such time as the

---

[96] Paragraph 8(2) of Schedule 1 to the 1982 Act

renewal application is determined (either by the licensing committee or, if appealed, by the Sheriff Court)[97].

7.43 It cannot be overstated that it is imperative a licence-holder knows the date of the expiry of the existing licence, and has taken steps to apply for a renewal of that licence. A failure to do so will mean that the existing licence lapses, the licence-holder will need to make a fresh application, but will in the meantime need to cease short-term let activities (with the financial and reputational damage that entails) or risk facing criminal prosecution for operating an unlicensed short-term let. The consequences of failing to follow the renewal application process are considerable.

7.44 The 2022 Order has also innovated upon the 1982 Act. Rather than confine renewal applications to a maximum period of three years, the 2022 Order permits local authorities to grant renewal applications (but not new applications) for a period of more than three years[98] (subject to the terms of its published licensing policy). That is to be commended. **Angus Council's policy** allows for the possibility that a licence might be renewed for a period of up to six years, whilst **Glasgow City Council** will permit a renewal for a period of five years where there has been no enforcement action during the period of the existing licence and no objections to the application for a renewed licence. **North Ayrshire Council**, in a trail blazing move, has set out a policy that would result in a licence being granted on an unlimited basis on payment of a recurring licensing fee every ten years (almost akin to a premises licence granted under the Licensing (Scotland) Act 2005). The licensing authority is to be commended for its bold approach. It reduces the burden on licensing committees and licence-holders (at a time when some licensing authorities are still trying to recover from the backlog of applications that arose during the Covid-19 pandemic, and at a time when the cost-of-

---

[97] Paragraph 8(5) of Schedule 1 to the 1982 Act
[98] Paragraph 10 of Schedule 2 to the 2022 Order

living crisis is putting significant pressure on applicants and licence-holders – pressure that is not helped by the cost of regulatory compliance with the new licensing scheme). As bold as the licensing authority has been, it is difficult to see that approach being enthusiastically adopted by other licensing authorities.

Deemed grant of a licence application

7.45 A very brief word on deemed grants of licence applications. What is set out above in respect of the licence application process presumes that an application is determined by a licensing authority in a timely manner. Given the anticipated numbers of short-term let licence applications, with the potential to overwhelm licensing authorities, it can be reasonably predicted that processing these new licence applications will take time. However, licensing authorities have only a limited period of time prescribed by statute within which to process and determine a licence application.

7.46 In respect of applications received from existing hosts prior to 1 April 2023 (which, it is assumed, will be amended to refer to 1 October 2023), licensing authorities must reach a final decision on the application within 12 months from the date the application was lodged[99]. For all other applications, the licensing authority must consider and reach a final decision on the application within 9 months from the date the application was lodged[100]. If the licensing authority fails to reach a final decision within the prescribed time periods, the application is deemed to be granted (or renewed or varied, etc)[101]. A licence that has been granted under these deemed provisions will remain in force for

---

[99] Article 7(2) of the 2022 Order

[100] Section 3(1) and (2) of the 1982 Act

[101] Section 3(4) of the 1982 Act

the period of one year[102]. In order to avoid the circumstance in which a licence is deemed to have been granted, a licensing authority can apply to the Sheriff Court, by way of summary application, requesting that the Sheriff extend the statutory deadlines, and the Sheriff may extend that period if he thinks there is good reason to do so[103].

7.47   It will be recalled that all hosts must have a licence in place to take bookings and receive guests by 1 July 2024. It is difficult to envisage how this deadline is practically achievable when licensing authorities also must reach a final decision within 12 months on an application lodged by an existing host prior to 1 October 2023. If an existing host were to wait until 20 September 2023 to lodge an application, a licensing authority (in terms of the 2022 Order as presently worded) should have until September 2024 to make a final decision on the application. That is plainly beyond the 1 July 2024 deadline. Perhaps what is more likely is that when the Scottish Government seeks to obtain legislative approval for the extension for existing hosts to apply for a licence (from 31 March 2023 to 30 September 2023), the Scottish Government will also make such minor amendments to the 2022 Order as are necessary to ensure all of the relevant timescales properly fit together.

Changes and alterations

7.48   As will also be referred to in Chapter 8 (concerning compliance and criminal liability), it is important for any licence-holder to be aware of his or her ongoing obligations to keep the licensing authority informed as to any material change in circumstance affecting the licence-holder, the short-term let activity, or the premises. In such circumstances, the licence-holder must notify

---

[102] Section 3(4A) of the 1982 Act

[103] Section 3(2) of the 1982 Act

the licensing authority as soon as reasonably practicable[104] (it is not for the licensing authority to attempt to police and monitor the issue). If a material change is to be made to the premises, the licence-holder must obtain the consent of the licensing authority (who, in turn, will consult with Police Scotland and the Scottish Fire and Rescue Service) before the change is made[105]. It will come as no surprise that such a notification to the licensing authority will also need to be accompanied by whatever fee the licensing authority has set for a material change in circumstances.

7.49 What is or is not a material change of circumstances is plainly a subjective decision of the licence-holder. That includes any material change to information that was provided to the licensing authority as part of the grant or renewal of a licence (for example, physical alterations to the premises, increasing the occupancy capacity, increasing the number of rooms available to guests, etc). Although plainly a subjective decision, it is nevertheless important to get the decision to notify correct. That is because a failure to notify a change in circumstances that a licensing authority does consider to be a material change would be a breach of paragraph 9 of Schedule 1 to the 1982 Act, and could be a matter that might weigh in the balance as to whether the licence-holder is a fit and proper person to hold a licence.

Surrender of the licence

7.50 Little needs to be said about surrender of a licence (generally speaking, once a licence has been surrendered the licence shall cease to have effect) in the context of a chapter dealing with the application process, other than to highlight an innovation to the 1982 Act that has been made by the 2022 Order. Indeed, this is an innovation that is to the benefit of hosts who may have second thoughts about the decision to surrender!

---

[104] Paragraph 9(1) to Schedule 1 of the 1982 Act

[105] Paragraph 9(2) to Schedule 1 of the 1982 Act

7.51   Where a holder of a short-term let licence has surrendered the licence, a licensing authority may grant an equivalent licence to the person who surrendered the licence if it receives an application within 12 months of the date of the surrender in respect of the same premises[106]. The licensing authority is permitted to re-issue the licence without going through the normal application process, consultation, and the giving of notice (since the licensing authority is essentially returning the licensing position to what it was had the licence-holder not surrendered the licence in the first place).

Public register

7.52   That there is to be a public register of short-term let licence-holders may not really matter to the vast majority of hosts. It is also to the credit of the consultation process (and I suspect the majority of stakeholders will not have a lot of positive things to say about the consultation or the 2022 Order!) that the personal details of individual licence-holders will not now be published as part of that public register.

7.53   The statutory position is that a licensing authority shall cause to be kept a register of applications as regards the receipt of each application and the final decision on each application. The register shall include a note of the kind and terms of each licence granted by the licensing authority and a note of any suspension, variation of the terms, revocation or surrender, of a licence[107].

7.54   Where the application is made by or on behalf of a person other than an individual (a natural person), the register will require to include the full name of the person, and the address of its registered or principal office.

---

[106] Paragraph 12 to Schedule 2 of the 2022 Order
[107] Paragraph 14 of Schedule 1 to the 1982 Act

7.55 In respect of all applications, the register will require to include:

(a) the full address of the premises which are the subject of the application (including a postcode),

(b) the council ward in which the premises are located,

(c) the date of the application,

(d) the status of the application (granted, refused, being determined, revoked, lapsed etc.),

(e) the type of premises,

(f) the type of short-term let,

(g) the maximum number of guests permitted to reside on the premises,

(h) whether the premises are within either Loch Lomond and the Trossachs National Park or the Cairngorms National Park,

(i) the unique licence number allocated to the application,

(j) where the licensing authority has required its inclusion in the application— the number of bedrooms in the premises, information on availability and occupancy, contact details for the manager of the premises, if different from the applicant or where the application is for secondary letting, and the Energy Performance Certificate rating.[108]

7.56 In short, very detailed information! Not only that, from 1 October 2022, the licensing authority must on a quarterly basis share the content of the register, in relation to short-term let

---

[108] Paragraph 13 of Schedule 2 to the 2022 Order

licences, with the Scottish Ministers in order for the information to be analysed[109].

Giving of Reasons[110]

7.57   Licensing authorities do not, as a matter of routine, give written reasons for each and every decision that is taken on applications that come before the authority. However, in respect of a prescribed list of decisions, the licensing authorities are obliged to produce written reasons if, within 21 days of the date of the decision, a request for reasons is made to the licensing authority by (as the case may be) the applicant, the licence-holder, an objector or other person heard by the licensing authority, the chief constable, or the Scottish Fire and Rescue Service.

7.58   The decisions of the licensing authority for which reasons may be requested include a decision:-

- to grant or renew a licence (or to refuse to do so);

- to revoke a licence (or to refuse to do so);

- to consent, or to refuse to consent, to a material change in any premises;

- to vary or refuse to vary the terms of a licence;

- to refuse an application for a temporary exemption, or to grant such an application subject to conditions;

- to serve an enforcement notice;

---

[109] Paragraph 13(c) of Schedule 2 to the 2022 Order, as it amends paragraph 14 of Schedule 1 to the 1982 Act

[110] Paragraph 17 of Schedule 1 to the 1982 Act

- to suspend a licence (immediately or otherwise) or to refuse to do so, or as to the period of suspension.

7.59 The written reasons given by a licensing authority do not need to be examples of great literary work. Similarly, reasons do not need to be unnecessarily verbose, nor do reasons need to attempt to be a transcript of every word that was said during the licensing hearing. That is not to say reasons are permitted to be so succinct as to render the reasons meaningless or unintelligible. Instead, it is a well-established principle of Scottish law that the decision of the licensing authority must "leave the informed reader and the court in no real and substantial doubt as to what the reasons for it were and what were the material considerations which were taken into account in reaching it"[111]. Put another way, whilst the written reasons may not be a detailed account of every point that was argued at the hearing, the reasons should engage with the material issues that arose for determination by the authority. The reasons should not just be a commentary of what was said at the hearing. If the licensing authority was tasked with balancing competing interests in favour, or against, the grant of a licence, then the reasons should explain *how* the licensing authority went about its decision-making task.

Appeals

7.60 There are a number of decisions that may be taken by a licensing committee in respect of a licence that carry with it a right of appeal. We are primarily concerned here with a decision to refuse a licence application, but the principle as to what follows would apply equally in respect of an appeal against any of the decisions referenced in the section above for which reasons can be sought.

7.61 An important pre-requisite of the entitlement to appeal against a decision of the licensing authority is that the person concerned

---

[111] *Wordie Property Co Limited v Secretary of State for Scotland* 1984 SLT 345 at 348.

has followed all such procedures for stating his case to the authority as have been made available to him[112]. What that means is that if an applicant does not take advantage of the opportunity to be heard by the licensing authority at a hearing on the application, or perhaps takes no steps to offer a counter argument to any objection or representation against the application, then the applicant could lose the entitlement to appeal. In practical terms, it is important to make sure that an applicant attends a hearing on the application and fully states his case to the licensing authority in support of that application.

7.62 In as much as a licensing committee hearing might be a relatively informal event, an appeal is lodged with the local Sheriff Court and is a very formal type of proceedings. An appeal against a decision to refuse a licence application will proceed by way of what is known as a summary application. Legal advice should be sought at an early stage in this regard. That is because the timescales are tight. An appeal can only be made if it is lodged with the Sheriff Court within 28 days (unless good cause is shown) from the date the application was refused[113].

7.63 The proceedings before the Sheriff Court are not a complete re-hearing of the licence application. This is not the licence-holder's chance to get a second chance at running arguments on the merits of the specific application. Rather, the powers of the Sheriff are (relatively) constrained. An appeal of this sort, rather than being a re-hearing of the application or evidence, is more a case of the Sheriff conducting a review as to how the licensing committee reached the decision it did (albeit the Sheriff may hear evidence as it is relevant to the grounds of appeal). It is not the purpose of this book to examine potential grounds of appeal in detail, but it is enough to highlight that a sheriff may uphold an appeal only if

---

[112] Paragraph 18(2) of Schedule 1 to the 1982 Act
[113] Paragraph 18(4) and (5) of Schedule 1 to the 1982 Act

he considers that the licensing authority, in arriving at their decision:

- erred in law (that is to say, the licensing authority exceeded its statutory powers under the 1982 Act, or acted in breach of the 1982 Act, or misinterpreted or misapplied any of the provisions under the 1982 Act);

- based their decision on any incorrect material fact (that is to say, that not only did the licensing authority base its decision on a fact that can be shown to be incorrect, but that the incorrect fact was material to the decision complained of);

- acted contrary to natural justice (that is to say, whether the licensing authority has dealt fairly and equally with the parties before reaching its decision on the application, and that there has been no procedural irregularity or unfairness); or

- exercised their discretion in an unreasonable manner (that is to say, the licensing authority has reached a decision that is so unreasonable that no reasonable licensing authority could have reached it)[114].

7.64 Appeal proceedings (even summary application proceedings) in Scotland can be a lengthy business, measured in months if not in excess of a year. As a consequence, a power is open to the Sheriff[115], when considering an appeal against the suspension or revocation of a licence, to order recall of the licensing authority's decision to suspend/revoke a licence (on an *interim* basis) pending the final determination of the appeal. If an appellant is able to successfully persuade the Sheriff that a decision to suspend

---

[114] Paragraph 18(7) of Schedule 1 to the 1982 Act

[115] Paragraph 18(10) of Schedule 1 to the 1982 Act

or revoke a licence should be recalled on a temporary (*interim*) basis, that at least assists the appellant with business continuity and would permit the licence-holder to continue with his licensable activity until such times as the Sheriff reaches a decision on the merits of the appeal.

7.65 Paragraph 18 of Schedule 1 to the 1982 Act also prescribes what course of action the Sheriff may take at the conclusion of the appeal proceedings and after the Sheriff has carefully considered all of the arguments. Of course, he may refuse the appeal. Alternatively, the Sheriff may find in favour of the appellant and uphold the appeal. If so doing, the Sheriff may remit the case with the reasons for his decision to the licensing authority for reconsideration of their decision, or reverse or modify the decision of the authority. In short, either the Sheriff takes the decision himself, or he sends the application back to the licensing authority for reconsideration of their decision.

7.66 There are two final procedural points to be aware of. Firstly, following the conclusion of the appeal, any party to an appeal under this part of the 1982 Act may further appeal on a point of law to the Court of Session. Again, the deadline for doing so is 28 days from the date of the Sheriff's decision[116]. Secondly, and perhaps more importantly, the Sheriff may make an order as to the expenses (costs) of the appeal as is appropriate. This is a significant consideration for any would-be appellant. Whilst the costs of attending a licensing authority hearing are relatively modest (generally whatever outlays the applicant may have, including the instruction of a licensing practitioner if required), the costs in litigating an appeal to the Sheriff Court can be considerable. The legal expenses will likely be a four-figure, if not a five-figure, sum of money. Although the appellant may be able to recover a proportion of those costs from the opposing side (usually the licensing committee) if he is successful, the reverse is

---

[116] Paragraph 18(12) of Schedule 1 to the 1982 Act

also painfully true – if an appellant commences an appeal but loses, he is not only liable for his own legal costs, but a proportion of the legal costs of his opponent. Appeal proceedings can become very expensive, very quickly, and should not be embarked upon without careful consideration as to the merits of any appeal.

CHAPTER EIGHT

COMPLIANCE

Introduction

8.1 Whilst this book is more about understanding the short-term let licensing scheme, and getting it right during the application process, it would be remiss not to briefly look at what enforcement options are available to the authorities if a premises is found to be non-compliant (either because it has a licence but has breached the terms of the licence, including the mandatory/additional conditions, or because it has no licence at all!).

8.2 As with many forms of civic enforcement, your local authority may visit your property to follow up on complaints (most likely from neighbours and/or guests!) and previous visits or as part of a routine pattern of inspection. Although your local authority must give notice ahead of routine visits, it is entitled to make unannounced inspections at any time to ensure you are adhering to your licensing conditions. It is recognised in the Guidance that it is far preferable for licensing authorities to seek to resolve complaints through dialogue with the host or operator in the first instance before seeking to invoke the more formal powers that exist under the 1982 Act[117].

What might enforcement look like?

8.3 Although it is possible that a licensing authority might seek to impose further additional conditions on a licence (through the variation of that licence), if matters have escalated because the issue is sufficiently serious then a licensing officer/licensing

---

[117] Para 6.3, Part 2 of the Guidance

authority will be looking at the following potential resolutions (in increasing order of severity):

(a) Enforcement notice

(b) Variation, suspension, or revocation of the licence

(c) Prosecution.

Enforcement Notices

8.4　The 2022 Order introduces a new paragraph 10A to Schedule 1 of the 1982 Act. That provision grants the power to licensing authorities to issue enforcement notices.

8.5　This means that where a licensing authority considers that any condition included in a short-term let licence has been breached (for example, from complaints, site visits or other information), or is likely to be breached (for example, it is apparent from a listing that the maximum occupancy being advertised is for six guests when the property is only licensed for three guests), then a licensing authority may serve an enforcement notice on a holder of a licence.

8.6　The enforcement notice will need to tell the licence-holder what has gone wrong, what action needs to be taken to make it right, and the deadline for so doing. If action is not taken to remedy the matters specified in the enforcement notice by the stipulated deadline, then the licensing authority will be empowered to vary, suspend or revoke the licence.

Variation, suspension or revocation of the licence

8.7　Generally once all other enforcement options have been exhausted, the licensing authority has the power to vary, suspend or revoke a short-term let licence. These steps may be taken if the licence-holder has been given time to put things right but has failed to do so.

8.8 However, it is not always the case that a licence-holder would first need to be served with an enforcement notice. If the allegation is sufficiently serious (for example, guests are at risk of serious harm), then the licence could be suspended or revoked without an enforcement notice having first been served if the circumstances justify it.

8.9 The licensing authority has incredibly broad discretion as to whether a term of a licence should be varied (at any time, on any grounds the licensing authority sees it, on an application made by the licence-holder, or on its own initiative), provided that the licensing authority has first given the licence-holder an opportunity to be heard in connection with the proposed variation[118]. Insofar as a licensing authority may consider the suspension or revocation of the licence, paragraph 11 to Schedule 1 of the 1982 Act is more specific as regards the grounds on which the licensing authority may suspend or revoke a licence:

> (a) the holder of the licence...is not or is no longer a fit and proper person to hold the licence;
>
> (b) the activity to which the licence relates is being managed by or carried on for the benefit of another person (other than the licence-holder), who would have been refused the grant or renewal of the licence;
>
> (c) there is an undue public nuisance issue or a threat to public order or public safety issue;
>
> (d) a condition of the licence has been contravened.

8.10 It will be apparent that the grounds on which the licensing authority may suspend or revoke a licence are derived from the grounds on which a licence application may be refused. In considering whether to suspend or revoke a licence, the licensing

---

[118] Paragraph 10 to Schedule 1 of the 1982 Act

authority may have regard to any misconduct on the part of the licence-holder which (in the opinion of the licensing authority) would have a bearing on their fitness to hold a licence. The licensing authority may also have regard to any misconduct on the part of persons frequenting or using the premises (whether that misconduct is on the premises or in the immediate vicinity)[119]. In considering whether or not to suspend or revoke a licence, the licensing authority shall give the holder of the licence, and complainer, and representatives of Police Scotland and Scottish Fire and Rescue Service (as appropriate) an opportunity to be heard in relation to the matters before the licensing authority[120]. The licensing authority must also act in a proportionate manner – a balance is to be struck between the alleged conduct in question, any other relevant materials before the licensing authority, and any plea-in-mitigation that is made by the licence-holder.

8.11 It is possible that a licensing authority may take the view that a licence requires to be suspended or revoked and the circumstances giving rise to that conclusion are so sufficiently serious (perhaps a serious and immediate risk to guest safety) that the licence should be suspended or revoked *immediately*[121].

8.12 If the licensing authority does not order an immediate suspension or revocation, then the suspension (for the unexpired portion of the duration of the licence, or such shorter period as the licensing authority may fix) or revocation of the licence will take effect once the period for an appeal to be lodged (28 days) has expired (or, if an appeal has been lodged, on the conclusion of the appeal proceedings)[122].

---

[119] Paragraph 11(4) of Schedule 1 to the 1982 Act

[120] Paragraph 11(7) of Schedule 1 to the 1982 Act

[121] Paragraph 11(10) of Schedule 1 to the 1982 Act

[122] Paragraph 11(9) of Schedule 1 to the 1982 Act

8.13   The licence may be suspended while the licensing authority considers a revocation. If the licence is revoked, it is important to understand that the licence-holder will be unable to make a further application in respect of the property for 12 months.

Criminal liability

8.14   Whilst many enforcement bodies will seek to resolve matters either informally, or exercising only civil enforcement powers, there will be circumstances in which hosts and operators may be prosecuted for alleged criminal offences (perhaps where the allegation itself is sufficiently serious, or there has been a repeated pattern of non-compliance for which civil enforcement has not had the desired effect).

8.15   There are four principal offences, and these can be found in section 7 of the 1982 Act. They are:

   (a) Operating without a licence

   (b) Failing to comply with a licence condition

   (c) Failing to notify a change

   (d) Making a false statement.

8.16   Whilst I set out below what the current maximum fine is following a successful prosecution, it is important to be aware that the Scottish Government's stated position is that it will (in some cases) seek to increase the maximum possible fine and so act as a significant and substantial deterrent to those who wilfully or deliberately fail to comply with the new licensing scheme.

Operating without a licence

8.17   Section 7(1) of the 1982 Act provides (insofar as is relevant to short-term letting) that:

> *Any person who without reasonable excuse does anything for which a licence is required under any provision of Part II of this Act…without having such a licence shall be guilty of an offence and liable, on summary conviction… to a fine not exceeding level 4 on the standard scale.*

8.18 Level 4 on the standard scale means £2,500. However, the Scottish Government intention is to seek to increase the maximum fine to £50,000.

Failing to comply with a licence condition

8.19 This offence is provided for in terms of section 7(2) of the 1982 Act, which states:

> *If a condition attached to a licence is not complied with, the holder of the licence shall…be guilty of an offence and liable, on summary conviction…to a fine not exceeding level 3 on the standard scale.*

8.20 What level 3 on the standard scale means in real terms is a maximum fine of £1,000. The majority of individuals reading this book might consider that to be a very modest maximum fine that perhaps does not have a lot of teeth to it. You would be correct. One example of breaching a licence condition would be to exceed the maximum occupancy capacity – a breach of that condition over an extended period of time would lead to significant financial reward for the offender. For that reason, the Scottish Government intention is to increase the maximum fine to £10,000.

8.21 It is also noteworthy that section 7(2) is not a strict liability offence (breach of the condition is, of itself, not a criminal offence). Rather section 7(3) provides that *it shall be a defence for a person charged with an offence under subsection (2) above to prove that he used all due diligence to prevent the commission of the offence.*

8.22 What that means is that if the licence-holder has his paperwork in order, or can demonstrate an audit trail as to decision-making, all of which tends to show that the licence-holder has done his best to comply with the licence condition, then it is likely that a successful defence (if the licence-holder were to be ultimately prosecuted) could be made out and a criminal conviction avoided.

8.23 This form of defence in a licensing context is not novel. One need only look to alcohol licensing that is regulated by the Licensing (Scotland) Act 2005. That too provides for a due diligence defence to certain alleged offences, such as the sale of alcohol to a minor. The language of section 141A of that Act is in almost identical terms to section 7(3). Having evidence of training documents and contract documents, and being able to credibly explain how the statutory provision had complied with, will allow for the possibility of a due diligence defence being advanced[123].

Making a false statement

8.24 Section 7(4) of the 1982 Act states that:

> *Any person who, in making an application under this Part of this Act to the licensing authority, makes any statement which he knows to be false or recklessly makes any statement which is false in a material particular shall be guilty of an offence and liable, on summary conviction…to a fine not exceeding level 4 on the standard scale.*

8.25 It was mentioned elsewhere in this book that a serious example of making a false statement would be to claim to be living at the premises (and so apply for a home-sharing short-term let licence) when, in fact, the person did not do so but made the deliberately false statement so as to avoid what will be the more challenging process of securing a secondary letting licence.

---

[123] *The Epic Group Scotland Limited v Procurator Fiscal, Aberdeen* [2014] HCJAC 20

8.26 Given the economic reward to the individual for successfully making the false statement is significant, the Scottish Government intention is to increase the maximum fine to £10,000.

Failing to notify a change

8.27 It is important to be aware that you must continue to update the relevant local authority where your circumstances change[124]. If you make physical alterations to your property, increase your number of guests or rooms, or change your property management company you must notify the relevant local authority as soon as possible.

8.28 In some cases, you may also require to seek the local authority's consent before making the change.

8.29 You will commit an offence if you fail to notify the local authority or fail to seek their approval where you require it.

8.30 Section 7(5) of the 1982 Act states that:

Any person who, being the holder of a licence—

(a) fails without reasonable excuse to notify the licensing authority of a 'material change of circumstances in accordance with paragraph 9(1) of Schedule 1 to this Act;

(b) without reasonable excuse makes or causes or permits to be made any material change in any premises, vehicle or vessel in contravention of paragraph 9(2) of Schedule 1 to this Act;

---

[124] Paragraph 9 to Schedule 1 of the 1982 Act

> (c) *fails without reasonable excuse to deliver his licence to the licensing authority in accordance with paragraph 13(2) of Schedule 1 to this Act,*
>
> *shall be guilty of an offence and liable, on summary conviction, to a fine not exceeding, in the case of an offence under paragraph (a) or (b) above, level 3 on the standard scale, and in the case of an offence under paragraph (c) above, level 1 on the standard scale.*

Further consequences

8.31   There are two further provisions of section 7 that potential applicants or licence-holders will want to be aware of.

8.32   The first concerns any further consequences on a successful conviction. Whilst the primary consequence is ending up with a criminal record and having a fine imposed, it should also be borne in mind that where a holder of a licence is convicted of an offence under section 7, the court may, in addition to any other financial penalty imposed, make an order that the licence shall be revoked and/or that the holder of the licence shall be disqualified from holding a licence for a period not exceeding 5 years[125].

8.33   The second concerns the question of the wider liability of the joint licence-holder. Where the offence alleged to have been committed is that of failing to comply with a licence condition by an employee or agent named in a licence, criminal proceedings in respect of that offence may be commenced not only against the employee/agent but also against the joint licence-holder (who is the employer of the employee or principal of the agent)[126]. So, in circumstances where there are joint licence-holders, it is not enough for one licence-holder to say he thought the other licence-holder was attending to compliance with the licence conditions – if there has been a breach, both licence-holders may have

---

[125] Section 7(6) of the 1982 Act

[126] Section 7(10) of the 1982 Act

criminal proceedings taken against them! (but, that would also be subject to the extent a due diligence offence can be made out).

Practical considerations

8.34 As is often the way with these things, it is better to be on the front foot in dealings with enforcement authorities.

8.35 It has already been mentioned elsewhere that complying with the mandatory conditions will require a degree of diligence on the part of a licence-holder, in particular ensuring the necessary gas, fire and electrical safety certificates and reports are kept up-to-date. For similar reasons, it will be just as important to take steps to be kept up-to-date with any changes to legislation or guidance that may impact upon the running of the short-term let. Ignorance of the law will not be an excuse!

8.36 If a licence-holder is aware that there is a problem with the property (or a part of the property) then it is plainly better to take the initiative and proactively take the property (or part of the property) out of service from guests. If, for whatever reason, the whole property has become unsafe or unsuitable for guests, then the licence-holder is really left with only one option (not to advertise the property, or take bookings, or receive guests). However, if the issue is confined to, say, one bedroom, then it may be possible (provided that good judgment is exercised) to take the one, unsafe room out of service, provided the remaining rooms that are available to guests remain safe and the licence conditions are being otherwise complied with.

8.37 In circumstances where a property has experienced issues (be that safety issues, or perhaps anti-social behaviour by guests), it would be prudent to keep a written record of what was done (and when) by way of steps to rectify the problem. Such an audit trail can prove to be very helpful if the police or licensing officer were to knock-on the door in response to a complaint and wanted to understand the standards that had been set for guests, what action had been taken against guests, and whether the short-term let booking was terminated earlier in order to quickly resolve an issue (if it was sufficiently serious). Such an audit trail would also be extremely useful if the allegation was a breach of a licensing condition and you needed to rely on the due diligence defence (i.e. that you had done all that could be reasonably done in the circumstances – see the section above on criminal liability).

8.38 And finally, an often-overlooked aspect of civic licensing under the 1982 Act. A short-term let licence that is granted is specific to the licence-holder and not to the premises. So, as and when a licence-holder comes to sell the premises, the short-term licence cannot transfer with the sale, and the purchaser will need to make a fresh application to the licensing authority. One might compare and contrast that position with what happens under the Licensing (Scotland) Act 2005 – where a premises licence can be transferred (provided certain statutory conditions are complied with) from seller to purchaser without the need to apply for a new licence.

CHAPTER NINE

LOOKING TO THE FUTURE

9.1 This book was written at a time when licensing authorities were consulting upon, and implementing, short-term let licensing policies. The licensing scheme had only been open to accept applications for a couple of months. The licensing scheme was all very new, as hosts, operators, booking platforms, licensing officers, and practitioners were all seeking to navigate (at points) potentially complicated waters. Some of the practical considerations I have suggested may not come to pass; or newer, unexpected issues may have cropped up.

9.2 To the uninitiated, it might be thought that the number of sources of information (legislation, government guidance, legal commentary, and so on) was overwhelming – and so I have attempted, hopefully in a reasonable way, to bring together those various sources of information into one book that is helpful in providing practical guidance to those involved in this new form of civic guidance.

9.3 What lies ahead? There are three areas that are especially interesting in the short-term.

9.4 Firstly, what is unknown is whether the licensing scheme will remain shielded from legal challenge (at the time of writing, there was the threat of judicial review proceedings being taken by a group of operators against Edinburgh Council's licensing policy). Licensing authorities could be at risk of licensing policies being the subject of judicial review in a general sense. Licensing authorities might also find that specific licensing decisions are the subject of appeal to the Sheriff Court. Secondly, will more local authorities introduce short-term let control areas? If so, that will inevitably have a significant impact on secondary letting nationwide. It is interesting that the licensing policy for Fife Council (at paragraph 12.3) made reference to consideration of control areas for short-term lets being progressed as part of the evidence gathering stage of Fife Council's Local Development Plan review. Might Fife Council be next? Thirdly, what of the proposed National Planning Framework 4? Specifically where it sets out at Policy 30 a policy for tourism:

Development proposals for the reuse of existing buildings for short-term holiday letting will not be supported where the proposal will result in:

1. *An unacceptable impact on local amenity or the character of a neighbourhood or area; or*

2. *The loss of residential accommodation where such loss is not outweighed by demonstrable local economic benefits.*

9.5 This is a discussion for another day, but plainly further thought needs to be given as to what is meant by "unacceptable impact on local amenity" and how one is to possibly demonstrate the loss of residential accommodation being outweighed by "demonstrable local economic benefit". In its current form, Policy 30 comes across as impenetrable and unworkable in practice.

9.6 Separate to all of what is mentioned above, the Scottish Government intends to carry out a review of the implementation of the licensing scheme in the summer of 2023 (the precise date is being kept under review following the Scottish Government's decision to extend the deadline for existing hosts to make a licence application to 30 September 2023 – it might make sense for any such review to be carried out after that milestone). Political appetite may change in the next 12 months – when the practical and economic effects of the licensing scheme are more keenly felt (and this will be especially so if the impact of the new licensing scheme is to drive short-term let operators away from the short-term let sector – how then will festivals and events cope with an absence of short-term accommodation and, if tourist numbers decline, what effect does that have on the wider economy?). Will we start to see a softening of approach by the Scottish Government, if the "report card" after one year considers that the Government has gone too hard, too fast on the short-term let sector?

9.7 For the Scottish Government (in particular, given the licensing of short-term lets has been a key policy position for a considerable period of time) as well as hosts, operators, booking platforms, licensing authorities and practitioners, this is just the start of a journey. It remains to be seen in what direction the road takes it.

MORE BOOKS BY
LAW BRIEF PUBLISHING

A selection of our other titles available now:-

'A Practical Guide to Parental Alienation in Private and Public Law Children Cases' by Sam King QC & Frankie Shama
'Contested Heritage – Removing Art from Land and Historic Buildings' by Richard Harwood QC, Catherine Dobson, David Sawtell
'The Limits of Separate Legal Personality: When Those Running a Company Can Be Held Personally Liable for Losses Caused to Third Parties Outside of the Company' by Dr Mike Wilkinson
'A Practical Guide to Transgender Law' by Robin Moira White & Nicola Newbegin
'Artificial Intelligence – The Practical Legal Issues (2nd Edition)' by John Buyers
'A Practical Guide to Residential Freehold Conveyancing' by Lorraine Richardson
'A Practical Guide to Pensions on Divorce for Lawyers' by Bryan Scant
'A Practical Guide to Challenging Sham Marriage Allegations in Immigration Law' by Priya Solanki
'A Practical Guide to Legal Rights in Scotland' by Sarah-Jane Macdonald
'A Practical Guide to New Build Conveyancing' by Paul Sams & Rebecca East
'A Practical Guide to Defending Barristers in Disciplinary Cases' by Marc Beaumont
'A Practical Guide to Inherited Wealth on Divorce' by Hayley Trim
'A Practical Guide to Practice Direction 12J and Domestic Abuse in Private Law Children Proceedings' by Rebecca Cross & Malvika Jaganmohan
'A Practical Guide to Confiscation and Restraint' by Narita Bahra QC, John Carl Townsend, David Winch
'A Practical Guide to the Law of Forests in Scotland' by Philip Buchan
'A Practical Guide to Health and Medical Cases in Immigration Law' by Rebecca Chapman & Miranda Butler
'A Practical Guide to Bad Character Evidence for Criminal Practitioners by Aparna Rao
'A Practical Guide to Extradition Law post-Brexit' by Myles Grandison et al

'A Practical Guide to Hoarding and Mental Health for Housing Lawyers' by Rachel Coyle
'A Practical Guide to Psychiatric Claims in Personal Injury – 2nd Edition' by Liam Ryan
'Stephens on Contractual Indemnities' by Richard Stephens
'A Practical Guide to the EU Succession Regulation' by Richard Frimston
'A Practical Guide to Solicitor and Client Costs – 2nd Edition' by Robin Dunne
'Constructive Dismissal – Practice Pointers and Principles' by Benjimin Burgher
'A Practical Guide to Religion and Belief Discrimination Claims in the Workplace' by Kashif Ali
'A Practical Guide to the Law of Medical Treatment Decisions' by Ben Troke
'Fundamental Dishonesty and QOCS in Personal Injury Proceedings: Law and Practice' by Jake Rowley
'A Practical Guide to the Law in Relation to School Exclusions' by Charlotte Hadfield & Alice de Coverley
'A Practical Guide to Divorce for the Silver Separators' by Karin Walker
'The Right to be Forgotten – The Law and Practical Issues' by Melissa Stock
'A Practical Guide to Planning Law and Rights of Way in National Parks, the Broads and AONBs' by James Maurici QC, James Neill et al
'A Practical Guide to Election Law' by Tom Tabori
'A Practical Guide to the Law in Relation to Surrogacy' by Andrew Powell
'A Practical Guide to Claims Arising from Fatal Accidents – 2nd Edition' by James Patience
'A Practical Guide to the Ownership of Employee Inventions – From Entitlement to Compensation' by James Tumbridge & Ashley Roughton
'A Practical Guide to Asbestos Claims' by Jonathan Owen & Gareth McAloon
'A Practical Guide to Stamp Duty Land Tax in England and Northern Ireland' by Suzanne O'Hara
'A Practical Guide to the Law of Farming Partnerships' by Philip Whitcomb
'Covid-19, Homeworking and the Law – The Essential Guide to Employment and GDPR Issues' by Forbes Solicitors
'Covid-19 and Criminal Law – The Essential Guide' by Ramya Nagesh
'Covid-19 and Family Law in England and Wales – The Essential Guide' by Safda Mahmood

'A Practical Guide to the Law of Unlawful Eviction and Harassment – 2nd Edition' by Stephanie Lovegrove
'Covid-19, Brexit and the Law of Commercial Leases – The Essential Guide' by Mark Shelton
'A Practical Guide to Costs in Personal Injury Claims – 2nd Edition' by Matthew Hoe
'A Practical Guide to the General Data Protection Regulation (GDPR) – 2nd Edition' by Keith Markham
'Ellis on Credit Hire – Sixth Edition' by Aidan Ellis & Tim Kevan
'A Practical Guide to Working with Litigants in Person and McKenzie Friends in Family Cases' by Stuart Barlow
'Protecting Unregistered Brands: A Practical Guide to the Law of Passing Off' by Lorna Brazell
'A Practical Guide to Secondary Liability and Joint Enterprise Post-Jogee' by Joanne Cecil & James Mehigan
'A Practical Guide to the Pre-Action RTA Claims Protocol for Personal Injury Lawyers' by Antonia Ford
'A Practical Guide to Neighbour Disputes and the Law' by Alexander Walsh
'A Practical Guide to Forfeiture of Leases' by Mark Shelton
'A Practical Guide to Coercive Control for Legal Practitioners and Victims' by Rachel Horman
'A Practical Guide to Rights Over Airspace and Subsoil' by Daniel Gatty
'Tackling Disclosure in the Criminal Courts – A Practitioner's Guide' by Narita Bahra QC & Don Ramble
'A Practical Guide to the Law of Driverless Cars – Second Edition' by Alex Glassbrook, Emma Northey & Scarlett Milligan
'A Practical Guide to TOLATA Claims' by Greg Williams
'A Practical Guide to Elderly Law – 2nd Edition' by Justin Patten
'A Practical Guide to Responding to Housing Disrepair and Unfitness Claims' by Iain Wightwick
'A Practical Guide to the Construction and Rectification of Wills and Trust Instruments' by Edward Hewitt
'A Practical Guide to the Law of Bullying and Harassment in the Workplace' by Philip Hyland
'How to Be a Freelance Solicitor: A Practical Guide to the SRA-Regulated Freelance Solicitor Model' by Paul Bennett

'A Practical Guide to Prison Injury Claims' by Malcolm Johnson
'A Practical Guide to the Small Claims Track - 2nd Edition' by Dominic Bright
'A Practical Guide to Advising Clients at the Police Station' by Colin Stephen McKeown-Beaumont
'A Practical Guide to Antisocial Behaviour Injunctions' by Iain Wightwick
'Practical Mediation: A Guide for Mediators, Advocates, Advisers, Lawyers, and Students in Civil, Commercial, Business, Property, Workplace, and Employment Cases' by Jonathan Dingle with John Sephton
'The Mini-Pupillage Workbook' by David Boyle
'A Practical Guide to Crofting Law' by Brian Inkster
'A Practical Guide to Spousal Maintenance' by Liz Cowell
'A Practical Guide to the Law of Domain Names and Cybersquatting' by Andrew Clemson
'A Practical Guide to the Law of Gender Pay Gap Reporting' by Harini Iyengar
'A Practical Guide to the Rights of Grandparents in Children Proceedings' by Stuart Barlow
'NHS Whistleblowing and the Law' by Joseph England
'Employment Law and the Gig Economy' by Nigel Mackay & Annie Powell
'A Practical Guide to Noise Induced Hearing Loss (NIHL) Claims' by Andrew Mckie, Ian Skeate, Gareth McAloon
'An Introduction to Beauty Negligence Claims – A Practical Guide for the Personal Injury Practitioner' by Greg Almond
'Intercompany Agreements for Transfer Pricing Compliance' by Paul Sutton
'Zen and the Art of Mediation' by Martin Plowman
'A Practical Guide to the SRA Principles, Individual and Law Firm Codes of Conduct 2019 – What Every Law Firm Needs to Know' by Paul Bennett
'A Practical Guide to Adoption for Family Lawyers' by Graham Pegg
'A Practical Guide to Industrial Disease Claims' by Andrew Mckie & Ian Skeate
'A Practical Guide to Redundancy' by Philip Hyland
'A Practical Guide to Vicarious Liability' by Mariel Irvine
'A Practical Guide to Applications for Landlord's Consent and Variation of Leases' by Mark Shelton
'A Practical Guide to Relief from Sanctions Post-Mitchell and Denton' by Peter Causton

'A Practical Guide to Equity Release for Advisors' by Paul Sams
'A Practical Guide to Financial Services Claims' by Chris Hegarty
'The Law of Houses in Multiple Occupation: A Practical Guide to HMO Proceedings' by Julian Hunt
'Occupiers, Highways and Defective Premises Claims: A Practical Guide Post-Jackson – 2nd Edition' by Andrew Mckie
'A Practical Guide to Financial Ombudsman Service Claims' by Adam Temple & Robert Scrivenor
'A Practical Guide to Advising Schools on Employment Law' by Jonathan Holden
'A Practical Guide to Running Housing Disrepair and Cavity Wall Claims: 2nd Edition' by Andrew Mckie & Ian Skeate
'A Practical Guide to Holiday Sickness Claims – 2nd Edition' by Andrew Mckie & Ian Skeate
'Arguments and Tactics for Personal Injury and Clinical Negligence Claims' by Dorian Williams
'A Practical Guide to Drone Law' by Rufus Ballaster, Andrew Firman, Eleanor Clot
'A Practical Guide to Compliance for Personal Injury Firms Working With Claims Management Companies' by Paul Bennett
'RTA Allegations of Fraud in a Post-Jackson Era: The Handbook – 2nd Edition' by Andrew Mckie
'RTA Personal Injury Claims: A Practical Guide Post-Jackson' by Andrew Mckie
'On Experts: CPR35 for Lawyers and Experts' by David Boyle
'An Introduction to Personal Injury Law' by David Boyle

These books and more are available to order online direct from the publisher at www.lawbriefpublishing.com, where you can also read free sample chapters. For any queries, contact us on 0844 587 2383 or mail@lawbriefpublishing.com.

Our books are also usually in stock at www.amazon.co.uk with free next day delivery for Prime members, and at good legal bookshops such as Wildy & Sons.

We are regularly launching new books in our series of practical day-to-day practitioners' guides. Visit our website and join our free newsletter to be kept informed and to receive special offers, free chapters, etc.

You can also follow us on Twitter at www.twitter.com/lawbriefpub.

Printed by BoD"in Norderstedt, Germany